Praise For Ken Goodman

My admiration is for his political acumen. Education does not just take place in classrooms. It is a political situation.

- **Frank Smith,** *University of Victoria, Canada*

I have found that with Ken and all his students they are driven by the same motivation. It is about making learning to read barrier free

- **Brian Cambourne,** *University of Wollongong, Australia*

His main contribution is freedom for teachers.

- **Jeanne Chall,** *Harvard University*

The whole language movement has to be counted as a popular success in winning the minds and hearts of teachers – certainly belief in the power and value of involvement, natural involvement in written language.

- **Richard Anderson,** *University of Illinois*

The idea of participation and collaboration is so much a part of what Ken has created within the field ... we learned that if we were ready to take risks, we would discover something powerful and new.

- **Carolyn Burke,** *Indiana University*

Ken's research is the kind of research that teachers can understand, because they've lived through listening to kids read real material, and kids trying to tell what they have read.

- **Dorothy Watson,** *University of Missouri Kansas City*

I think Ken has done a lot of good in bringing these ideas before people.... I can't think of anyone who has been more influential in classrooms.

- **Ira Aaron,** *University of Georgia*

I think Ken is a really good person, and by that I mean, a good representative of the efforts that were being made to bring psychology out of the era of behaviorism. ... What Ken did was to get us to examine our own positions and our own terminology.

- **S. Jay Samuels,** *University of Minnesota*

To me in 1968-69 what I found so powerful in his message, from a humanistic perspective, was giving kids credit for what they do. ... He was really a hero for me. There was this researcher who was evoking these views of reading as a language process, which was so refreshing and exciting.

- **P. David Pearson,** *University of California Berkeley*

I remember talking to Ken and Yetta about our personal contributions. We said that if we looked back at some time in our lives we hoped there would be fifty or a hundred graduate students who took what we did and took it further and I think that is one of the great contributions of their lives.

- **Roger Shuy,** *Georgetown University*

Ken is a carefully principled person. I think the essence of his work is the ethical and the moral dimensions that we haven't explored. I'm defining moral as the kinds of values that bind relationships between teachers and children…that have moral implications that are fundamental to the way in which we view foundations of education.

- **Jerome Harste,** *Indiana University*

One of the challenges was to give teachers voices. We were trying to change the ways in which we worked and talked. More and more committees were interested in interacting. In the midst of all this whole language burst on the scene.

- **Angela Jaggar,** *New York University*

I also remember that he brought in Emilia Ferreiro. Do you know how significant it is to bring in women of color who are pioneers? Ken and Yetta did that. I think their work has really been revolutionary throughout the world.

- **Barbara Flores,** *California State University*

I often think about where they fit in historically. Why Ken and Yetta were able to develop the theories as they did, and how their theories on reading will impact the future for teachers and kids.

- Bess Altwerger, *Towson University*

WHAT'S WHOLE IN WHOLE LANGUAGE IN THE 21ST CENTURY?

KEN GOODMAN

GARN PRESS
NEW YORK, NY

WHAT'S WHOLE IN WHOLE LANGUAGE IN THE 21ST CENTURY?

KEN GOODMAN

NEW YORK, NY

Published by Garn Press, LLC
New York, NY
www.garnpress.com

Garn Press and the Chapwoman logo are registered trademarks of Garn Press, LLC

Copyright © 1986, 2005, 2014 by Kenneth Goodman

All rights reserved. No part of this publication may be reproduced, distributed, or transmitted in any form or by any means, including photocopying, recording, or other electronic or mechanical methods, without the prior written permission of the publisher, except in the case of brief quotations embodied in critical reviews and certain other noncommercial uses permitted by copyright law. For permission requests, please send an email to Garn Press addressed "Attention: Permissions Coordinator," at *permissionscoordinator@garnpress.com*

The interviews in *The 1992 -1993 Interviews of Renowned Reading Scholars* section of this book are copyright © 1992, 1993 by Denny Taylor and are used with permission.

Book and cover design by Ben James Taylor/Garn Press
Cover photo by Phil Marino for Hofstra University's 2011 Reading Miscue Analysis Conference, used with permission.

Library of Congress Control Number: 2014953459

Publisher's Cataloging-in-Publication Data

Goodman, Kenneth S.
    What's whole in whole language in the 21st century? / Ken Goodman.
        pages cm
    Original title: What's whole in whole language?
    ISBN: 978-1-942146-04-9 (pbk.)
    ISBN: 978-1-942146-05-6 (e-book)
        1. Language experience approach in education. 2. Children—Language.
3. English language—Study and teaching. 4. Teaching, Freedom of. 5. Public schools.
6. Democracy and education. I. Rosen, Michael. II. Taylor, Denny. III. Altwerger, Bess. IV. Meyer, Rick. V. Title: What's whole in whole language?
LB1575.8 .G65 2014
372.6—dc23
                              2014953459

This book is dedicated to Denny Taylor who, coincidentally, has republished this book. No one has been a more persistent voice for children, for the underprivileged, for teachers.

And no has been more persistent in advocating for sanity in this era of the pedagogy of the absurd. I'm proud to be associated with her in her new incarnation as publisher and proud to be her friend and colleague. Her research and advocacy have done much to inform educators, including me.

May her voice be heard above those who profit from tests, texts, and the immorality of sweatshop kindergartens and assembly-line schools.

Ken Goodman
October 2014

Acknowledgments

There are many who helped to make this book have the success it has had. Adrian Peetoom, my editor for the first version, was unique in encouraging my unconventional style and disdain for conformity. Roger Rapoport kept the book available in the dark ages of NCLB in the second publication. And Denny Taylor's Garn has brought it into the 21st century and provided added material to put in the context of its time and of these times.

And I want to give a shout out for all those teachers who have never lost their dedication to teaching and their pupils, and have quietly nodded their heads as they were told what they were to do and how they were to do it - and then closed their classroom doors and launched another group of pupils gloriously into literacy.

Thanks also to all my students, who decade by decade have kept me on my toes and made me proud to be a teacher. Thanks to my forever Yetta, and to my children, grandchildren and great grandchildren who provided so many literacy events for me to share while making my life so full and my finances so complex.

Table Of Contents

Welcome Back To *What's Whole In Whole Language?*   1

My Life And This Book   5

Whole Language: Is This The End Or A New Beginning?   11

Teachers As Reflective Practitioners: Achieving Social Justice And Equity   21

Preface To The 1986 Edition   37

Chapter 1: Whole Language: The Easy Way To Language Development   39

     What makes language learning hard?   42
     What makes language learning easy?   43

Chapter 2: Language: What And Why?   45

     What is language?   46
     Why is language important?   51

Chapter 3: Language Learning: How Does It Happen?   54

     Is written language different?   61

Chapter 4: School: A Whole Language View   64

What is the basis of whole language teaching?   65
A view of curriculum   71
What is a whole language classroom?   74

Chapter 5: Whole Language: What Makes It Whole?   77

What is not whole language?   77
Skills-technology views   78
What are the principles of whole language?   83
What's whole about whole language?   87

Chapter 6: Developing Literacy: Whole Language The Whole Way   90

How can whole language be implemented?   90
Preschool literacy   92
Beginning literacy   94
Developmental literacy   99

Chapter 7: Revaluing: An Alternative To Remediation   108

Chapter 8: Reality: The State Of The Language Arts   115

What is happening in whole language?   116
How can policy become practice?   121

Chapter 9: Whole Language: Not Without A Whole Language Teacher   129

What makes a whole language teacher?   130

Chapter 10: Afterword: Whole Language And The Pedagogy Of The Absurd   143

The 1992-1993 Interviews Of Renowned Reading Scholars   151

Denny Taylor: Hofstra University   153
Ken and Yetta Goodman: University of Arizona   155
Harold and Betty Rosen: London Institute of Education   159

Frank Smith: University of Victoria, Canada	162
Brian Cambourne: University of Wollongong, Australia	168
Jeanne Chall: Harvard University	172
Richard Anderson: University of Illinois	176
Carolyn Burke: Indiana University	178
Dorothy Menosky: New Jersey City University	183
Dorothy Watson: University of Missouri Kansas City	187
Rudine Sims Bishop: Ohio State University	191
Ira Aaron: University of Georgia	194
Richard Hodges: University of Chicago	197
Robert Shafer: Arizona State University	201
S. Jay Samuels: University of Minnesota	205
P. David Pearson: University of California Berkeley	210
Roger Shuy: Georgetown University	214
Jerome Harste: Indiana University	218
Angela Jaggar: New York University	223
Barbara Flores: California State University	227
Bess Altwerger: Towson University	233

Other Books By Ken Goodman   238

Michael Rosen

Welcome Back To
What's Whole In Whole Language?

In the present climate, it's become very hard for a voice to be heard reminding us that speaking, listening, reading and writing are all connected. How much easier to turn all this into separate "skills", each of which, it is believed, can be taught separately! How much easier then to test these skills separately too, and in so doing, grade and select children for different pathways through education, determined by these measurements - likewise the teachers and the schools.

Let's remember that these tests, which have so much bearing on what kind of education any given child is allowed to have, are not flawless windows into what a child can and can't do. So, when we hear that a six year old is or is not "reading" we have to ask what kind of test is producing this "fact"? And we find that it is a "reading aloud" test. Now, most of us would think of "reading" as a "whole" activity, where we make sense of some writing. Whatever it is that we need to do in order to "read aloud" it may or may not involve making sense of some writing. In other words, telling us that this or that child failed a "reading test" is not really true. The so-called objective statistics may not be telling us what we really need to know.

Then again, when we are told that the statistics tell us that a particular kind of skills-based method of teaching to read is out-performing all other methods, we are entitled to ask questions like: are you testing "whole" reading - that is, "reading with understanding"? Are you testing how children read with understanding three, four and five years down the track after these skill-based methods were used? Do you have any evidence to suggest that these skills-based methods help children make sense of what they're reading?

Now, when we broaden the matter out to such matters, we are then in the territory of asking questions like, what kinds of classrooms do we need to create to help children of all ages understand what they're reading? And when we ask this, we find ourselves back with speaking, listening, reading and writing. We find that talking about what we read and write is great for making sense of everything. We find that reading and writing about what we talk about is great for making another kind of sense. What's more, we start to talk about what children are saying and listening to outside the classroom. What kind of out-of-school activities are they involved with? How can parents best help their children? By doing replicas of the tests over and over, or by taking them to the library? Letting their children choose whatever they want and sitting listening to their children talk about what they're reading?

These are matters that we need to engage with urgently, if we don't want the education of our children to be a matter of narrowing down our children's options, in order to satisfy the urge to grade them every inch of the way. *What's Whole in Whole Language in the*

21st Century? takes us through the questions and issues involved. We need to be well-informed about this matter. In the American phrase that I've learned to love, "we need to wise up". This book helps us do just that.

Ken Goodman

My Life And This Book

Up until this book was published in 1986 I had become reasonably well known in educational circles, but I was of little or no interest either to the media or to any politician. I was an autoworker through summers in college except for 1948, when I left school to work for the election of Henry Wallace and worked full time in the Packard auto plant in Detroit. I represented my UAW local at the Young Progressives Convention in Philadelphia.

I taught eighth grade in Southern California after graduating from UCLA and getting a teaching certificate at brand new Cal State LA in 1949. In 1952 I married Yetta who I met working summers in Jewish Center day camps. At the end of the next school year I became a victim of McCarthyism. I left teaching involuntarily for several years working as a social group worker.

Eventually I took the risk of going back to UCLA for my doctorate in education. And so I found myself back in Detroit as an assistant professor at Wayne State University in 1962. I taught there for 15 years, during which I completed major funded studies on the reading process using miscue analysis. My research led to a life-long goal of developing a comprehensive theory of the reading process.

Yetta and I shared our understanding with teachers whenever we were invited to do so, often involving our amazing graduate students. Eventually I was elected to the Board of the International Reading Association and then President of IRA in 1980, shortly after Yetta was elected President of the National Council of Teachers of English.

In 1978 we took jobs together at the University of Arizona. For a period, our work was better known in Canada, Australia, New Zealand and Australia than in the US. In the United States it was treated as interesting but radical.

We were often in Winnipeg, Manitoba, where an interesting group of teachers had started to use the term whole language. The well-paid and well-educated Canadian teachers were rejecting the US preoccupation with textbooks and tests. They saw US language arts as fragmented and so began to call what they were doing "whole" language. They organized conferences for teachers that attracted several thousand, including a number from the States. The first edition of this little book grew out of a presentation I did in Winnipeg. I was invited to do a series of books for Scholastic Canada and this was the first, followed by *Phonics Phacts* and *Ken Goodman On Reading*.

Over the next several years *What's Whole in Whole Language?* sold over 250,000 copies in several languages. That paralleled the grass roots movement of teachers to whole language, who brought this sea change into their classrooms.

Now when I say I hadn't drawn the attention of media and politicians I don't mean to neglect some attention I got from ardent advocates of phonics and direct instruction in reading. They rejected our research and confused whole language with whole word and what they called "look and say".

I was also being frequently mentioned in the publications of a growing well-organized attempt to influence state and federal lawmakers to legislate the way reading should be taught. I was the focus of one part of a white paper issued by the Republican Caucus in the US Senate.

Things suddenly changed in 1994 when Art Levine, who I had never met, picked up phonics vs whole language from the phonics advocates and legitimatized it, making me the face of whole language in "A Revisiting the Great Debate" published in *Atlantic Monthly Magazine*. It was the beginning of what the media would call the "Reading Wars". Suddenly I was getting two to four calls a week from national as well as local media, interviewing me by phone and then posing me as the whole language guru.

I was personally to blame for millions of children failing to learn to read.

What was a growing grass roots movement toward whole language was being erroneously conflated as the long-term dominant method of teaching reading. And phonics was the one true scientific and sure way to teach reading, which had worked well until teachers were misled by Ken Goodman.

I began to examine where this sudden interest was coming from, and I came to realize that there was a very organized and well-funded campaign centered in the Heritage Foundation, the Manhattan Institute, and the Thomas B. Fordham Institute. They used reading to privatize public education with their money from right wing foundations and access to the major corporations that controlled the media, including school publishing.

Recently I became aware that I was the center of attention in a very surprising place. One day when I finished looking for the source of a quote I needed for references in the Google Book data base, I asked the program to look for "Ken Goodman crazy". Up came this: "I don't know why Ken Goodman is on this planet but I don't think it's to teach kids to read". That was Margaret Spellings, speaking in her office in the White House as the second George Bush's domestic advisor and who would become Secretary of Education, to Ronald Kessler, who was doing an authorized book on the Bush White House. The book, *A Matter of Character: Inside the White House of George W. Bush* was published in 2004, as part of the Bush re-election campaign.

I ordered a copy of the book. That's when I discovered I had received a great deal of attention in the White House in early 2001. Under the guidance of a group of , Bush had built his successful campaign for Governor of Texas by framing an anti-public school agenda around school reform to save minority students from illiteracy. The campaign worked very well in Texas, even getting a good share of Hispanic voters who bought the Bush's promise that he was doing something good for their kids. His advisors were Margaret Spellings, Karl Rove and Sandy Kress. They introduced him to Reid Lyon, who was a minor staffer at NICHD. They all went with him to Washington in some role.

The campaign worked so well in Texas that reading reform became the key promise of Bush's Presidential Campaign. It was Margaret Spellings who, on advice from her neoconservative think tank friends, said don't just make it about phonics. Let's call it scientifically based reading instruction.

When Bush moved into the White House the first piece of legislature on his agenda was rewriting the Elementary and Secondary Education Act as *No Child Left Behind (NCLB)*. George

Miller and Ted Kennedy were invited as leading Democrats in the House and Senate to join the effort. Kessler reports conversations with Spellings, Rove, Kress and Lyon in which he interweaves comments of a telephone interview with me I hardly remember. I certainly did not anticipate my prominent role in two chapters of a book on the Bush White House. According to Kessler, NCLB and reading reform would establish Bush as the "compassionate conservative".

By September 2001, NCLB had been rewritten with "scientifically based reading research" appearing over and over again as a euphemism for phonics. Bush would go to an inner city classroom to read a story to the children from the Distar program. And so there he was on the morning of September 11, 2001 launching NCLB to save children from –? Me.

That morning he learned of a bigger threat to America than whole language. He could leave reading to his trusted advisors. Now it is October 2014, the year in which, according to NCLB, all children would be reading. All that's been achieved is the dismantling of public education.

I retired from the University of Arizona in August, 1998, but I still had enough research, writing, and work with teachers to keep me busy for the rest of my life. And I will continue to advocate for Freedom to Learn, Freedom to Teach, and Social Justice.

Last year, Yetta and I, together with Bob Calfee, published *Whose Knowledge Counts in Government Literacy Policies?* And the current White House has not yet called for my advice.

Denny Taylor

Whole Language: Is This The End Or A New Beginning?

A young woman and a young man sit down next to me on a park bench overlooking the pond with miniature sail boats in Central Park. They talk about the production of a play.

"It's really fun to pretend," the young man says.

The young woman agrees.

"Do you read?" the young man asks.

The young woman laughs. "In university it's kind of a requirement."

The young man talks about Tumblr and says "You've got to throw yourself out there."

"When were you born?" the young woman asks.

"I was born in 1994," the young man says. "Yeh, it was a great year."

"Have you heard this theory that we are post future?" the young woman asks, without laughing at his "great year" joke.

"Nope."

"The future has happened in the 1990's," the young woman says.

She talks of books and movies that predicted the future that we have now lived, and I think of the lines from one of Rilke's poem, "I have seen for some time now, the change in everything" as I get up and walk on.

So many educators knew in the 1990's that our time was being taken away. The future was happening. Big corporations were aggressively targeting teachers. Capital-intensive US corporations represented by the Business Council and the Business Round Table were using PR firms' propaganda to realign the public's common understandings of the purpose of schools and of how young children learn to read and write.

At the beginning of the 1990's, a well-orchestrated effort in state-corporate cooperation was initiated to disenfranchise the growing influence of teachers at the local level across the US. Teachers were creating and using developmentally appropriate teaching-learning materials and activities in public schools that limited the influence of corporate curriculum producers.

School districts were spending money on real books instead of artificial, commercially produced programs, and there was concern about the growing rejection of commercial text-book producers, including McGraw-Hill, in the five big adoption states – Texas, California, Michigan, Florida, and New York. Textbooks and basal reading programs purchased by the big five were then purchased by the rest of the states, sometimes referred to as "territories".

Billions in revenues and profits were at stake. Profits dropped. Not a whole lot, but even a slight dip could be counted in the hundreds of millions and mount up to billions in a just a few years. Worse, the growing teacher-led democratic movement was taking hold, causing concern about displacement from the education markets of the powerful elites in government and big business. From studying the teacher movements of that time, I can write that teachers really believed that the ways in which they were teaching children in school would lead to a more just and equitable society.

The struggle was for a social democracy that fulfilled Martin Luther King's dream.

The business community of the corporate world needed a strategy that did not seem political. Big money and political power had to be protected. It was in this context that the "Reading Wars" were invented through a massive PR propaganda campaign and the well-orchestrated efforts of the media. What is long forgotten or perhaps never known is that, with the support of the Texas Business Round Table and the National Institute of Child Health and Human Development (NICHD), the "Houston Reading Studies" became a key component of the strategy.

So the grand plan to deceive the public was on. A study, seemingly "scientific", with the classroom manipulation of early reading instruction, was devised that would leave nothing to chance.

George W. Bush was Governor of Texas at the time of the Houston Reading Studies. The following quotes are taken from the transcript of the 1996 pre-summit meeting of then Governor Bush's Business Council.

"The design of the study is hopelessly complex," the principal researcher said. "If just looking at this gives you a headache, you'll know how I feel every day trying to monitor this."

The principal investigator talked about the commercial direct instruction program *Open Court*, published by McGraw-Hill, and then of the "whole language program", which was the second early reading approach in the comparative study. Her use of "program" locates the conversation in time, because whole language is considered a philosophy, an approach to teaching and learning that can be traced back to Montaigne in the sixteenth century, and stretching back to even earlier times. It is an approach to teaching and learning that is deeply rooted in the efforts of educators to expand human rights and social equality. It is also grounded in the research of eminent physicians and psychologists who studied child development, and in the research of renowned linguists, including Michael Halliday, who studied language development – how infants and small children learn language, learn *through* language, and learn *about* language.

What is important to take into consideration here is that Acts of Congress were based on the Houston Reading Studies. Hundreds of millions of dollars, and billions over time, in corporate revenues and profits counted on the findings. And yet the principal investigator, by her own admission, did not know anything about "whole language".

"I don't know what that means," the principal investigator said when she talked about whole language, adding that the project director did.

It gets worse.

"When the study started," the principal investigator said at the 1996 pre-summit meeting of then Governor Bush's Business Council, "the superintendent was fired for her whole language belief. The school board took over curriculum decisions and decided in the middle of our study that we should stop the study because in NIH when a drug works, you stop it, and everybody gets the good drug."

"And they had already decided that phonics worked," the principal investigator said, "so they wanted the whole district to have the phonics program. But we persisted and continued the study, but it's very difficult to do good research in these settings. There are too many stakeholders who know the answers before you start."

The study was too meaningless to deserve discussion, nothing more than a very bad example of political science, with nothing to be learned from it, except how the privileged elites manipulate the data as well as the public.

At the time of the Houston Reading Studies, Governor Bush declared his candidacy for the Presidency of the United States, and public education was central to his political campaign, which is why the outcome of the studies could not be left to chance. It must already be clear that this observation is not uniformed political speculation. I spent more than a year documenting the Houston Reading Studies at the time that they were taking place.

This research was ethnographic with: (1) information directly received about the study from teachers who were required to participate; and (2) copies of original documentation from the study during the analysis stage of the research. The data that I analyzed was the focus of the book, *Beginning to Read and the Spin Doctors of Science*.

The sources were not revealed in the book. But I can write that they were teachers of great intellectual stature and courage who have passed the baton to the teachers in today's resistant movement. Now, the sheer number of teachers, who are resisting the centralization of public education that is deleterious to children and US society, has made it possible for them to be more open in their dissent. But in public schools in Texas in the 1990's there were teachers who were truly frightened about the consequences of speaking out about the "research" that was taking place in public schools.

Many current parents and teachers would have been children when McGraw Hill funded the Houston Reading Studies that were conducted under the auspices of the NICHD. It is highly likely that some of today's parents were taught to read based on the fudged outcomes of those studies, just as their children are now. The Common Core and the testing regimes in place today are the lasting legacy of these discredited studies.

The Houston Reading Studies were designed from the outset to "prove" that children taught to read by McGraw Hill's *Open Court* Direct Instruction were significantly more successful than children who learned to read through a Whole Language approach. The evidence is compelling that the studies were not only invalid, but that the outcomes were deliberately "orchestrated".

The studies violated the conditions for scientific research commonly held in both the social and physical sciences, and across both quantitative and qualitative research paradigms. Ultimately, what many reading researchers knew then, and what has been borne out by subsequent events, is that the Houston Reading Studies were nothing more than an attention getting sideshow to distract the public from the real agenda of the Federal Government and Corporate America, which was to take away local control of US public school from cities and towns, from neighborhoods and communities, and most importantly, from teachers and parents.

The studies served their purpose. Texas Governor George W.

Bush was elected the "education president", and Harold McGraw, a longtime friend of the Bush family, saw a significant increase in revenues and profits for McGraw Hill's *Open Court*. It was, however, a sad day for the nation's children. The lasting impact on their lives has been and continues to be devastating.

The effects were systemic. In the late 1970's and 1980's the gap between rich and poor was closing; similarly the gap between different ethnic groups in school achievement was perceptibly less. Much of the educational research at that time focused on developing greater understanding of the social contexts in which young children learn to read and write, and in narrowing the disparities in educational opportunities for rich and poor, black and white, and being sensitive to the needs of other "minority" groups.

Teachers were focused on closing the gap, but the response from Washington was that you could have too much democracy. In 1998 the Republican controlled US Congress used the Houston Reading Studies as a basis for the *Reading Excellence Act*, which was the precursor to the 2002 *No Child Left Behind (NCLB) Act*. It was a critical blow to teachers whose pedagogical practices were developmentally appropriate, and who were part of the late 20th century civil rights movement for children. The NCLB Act put an end to the movement and left the survivors staggering.

"In January 2002, President George W. Bush signed the *No Child Let Behind Act* (NCLB; PL 107-110) instituting a major federal encroachment on public education in the United States," Robert Calfee writes, in an article with the subtitle, *How the Federal Government Used Science to Take Over Public Schools*.

"The focus is on literacy," Calfee, a Reading Hall of Fame scholar, writes, "but the implications are far reaching, and go to the core of the intersections of science and politics, of knowledge and power, and of the balance between federal and local control, as these affect the education of young children."

In recent years the discourse of power in public education has built many arguments that can be traced back to the falsified "scientific evidence" of the Houston Reading Studies that are harmful to the health and well-being of children, as well as damaging to their academic development.

What followed was a media blitz of PR generated distortions and lies, lauding the use of direct instruction and commercial reading programs. Teachers were denigrated and doubts spread about their socially sensitive, developmentally appropriate, pedagogical practices. Witched, teachers struggled to maintain their child centered classrooms even when they were under attack.

The verbiage was political PR pulp, which was spoon-fed by the corporate media to the public at the breakfast and dinner table. The original research that was fudged has been long forgotten, but the "findings" became the unquestionable truth of the George W. Bush presidential campaign and his later presidency, with the protests of teachers denigrated as some sort of mass social dementia.

The teacher-initiated movement to make schools more equitable was crushed. The vision faded of schools as places in which children were engaged in developmentally appropriate learning activities and inquiry projects that spanned the curriculum, combining every subject from science projects that incorporated the arts.

Today, few teachers or parents know this dystopian story of how the research or the findings of the Houston Reading Study were used to mandate that public schools purchase and use high-end, big budget, commercial reading programs and high stakes tests. This is the reason Garn Press is republishing *What's Whole in Whole Language?*, Ken Goodman's most remarkable book.

This 21st century edition of *What's Whole in Whole Language?*

is doubly remarkable, because it also contains interviews that were all conducted in 1992-93 of renowned reading scholars to document the professional lives and research of Ken and Yetta Goodman. These interviews provide profound insights into the reading research that was conducted in second half of the 20th century, before the lights went out on the vision of educators for a democratic society in which poverty and inequality could be eliminated. It was the mission of teachers to make public schools places where imagination and creativity were intertwined with great scholarship that pitted them against the political and corporate elites who were intent on increasing the centralization of wealth and power.

The interviews are gentle, kind, understanding of different perspectives on reading research, and of how young children learn to read and write. These are researchers who disagreed, but they were not at war. They respected one another. Above all they spoke with great admiration for the ethical and moral integrity of Ken and Yetta Goodman.

Rereading the 1992-93 interviews more than twenty years after they took place is an uncanny experience. The young woman sitting with the young man on the bench in Central Park comes to mind. I share her sense of living in a post future time, because it is very clear that the commentary of the great scholars who talked about the research of Ken and Yetta Goodman took place before, as Rilke wrote, "the change in everything."

Reading these interviews adds new dimensions and insights to the reading of *What's Whole in Whole Language in the 21st Century?* For teachers and for parents of children, who are being educated in public schools in this post-future dystopian age, the question is whether this remarkable little book, that is one of the most banned books in education, can make a difference to our shared vision of the future?

Is this the end or a new beginning?

Can Ken and Yetta Goodman, who are now so venerable, lead us to a new beginning in this tumultuous age? They very well might if teachers and parents read *What's Whole in Whole Language in the 21st Century?*

Bess Altwerger And Rick Meyer

Teachers As Reflective Practitioners: Achieving Social Justice And Equity

This mighty little book of less than one hundred pages in the original version became a handbook for the revolution that occurred in many classrooms around the world. Teachers were inspired to put aside materials that were based on a very limited understanding of reading and writing and, instead, place children and their very natural curiosity about language and learning at the center of classroom activity.

Ken Goodman had no connections to any corporations or other profit seekers when he authored this book; instead, he was interested in helping teachers and parents gain important insights into the very natural (and also quite remarkable) processes in which children engage in order to be literate. Rather than attempt to summarize or reiterate the lessons in this volume, we will, instead, provide two examples from our own teaching and research. These will serve to demonstrate the literacy teaching and learning that unfolded in the 1970's, 80's and 90's, when whole language teachers shifted their thinking to the languages and cultures that children brought to school, the ways in which they expressed themselves, and their desires to understand and actively participate in the literate world.

Bess: A Dig in Our Own Backyard

When I was working with teachers at an elementary school in Arizona to learn about and implement whole language in their classrooms, many local educators asked if they could visit the school to observe this new way of teaching.

One day, I escorted a group of visitors down the hallway toward Karen's Chapter I Resource room. Like previous visitors, I knew they expected to see a teacher standing in front of the room delivering a lesson on phonics, vocabulary or comprehension to a quiet class of "at risk" students.

The visitors expected to see colorful charts on phonics rules or common vocabulary words hanging on the walls and shelves of commercial reading materials. Maybe they expected to see the teacher meeting in a corner with one of her ability groups while the rest of the class was filling out worksheets at their seats.

I knew that if these visitors were expecting "whole language" to just be a new method of teaching reading, they were in for a big surprise. And they were. As they approached Karen's room, the hum of children's voices grew louder, but it sounded more like a concert than chaos.

Once in the room, the first thing the visitors noticed was that the arrangement of tables and desks were not in rows, but grouped in various corners of the room and that they were stacked high with books, art supplies, odd shaped black objects, and audio equipment. There was also a large empty space in the middle of the room where small groups of kids were sitting together with their heads bowed over some books, pointing to the pages and talking quietly. Chairs were arranged around some of the tables, but the visitors wondered aloud if there was an assigned seat for each child. And then came the question that I expected.

"Where's the teacher's desk?" they asked. "Where's the teacher?"

I looked around and pointed her out, crouching down to the height of second graders helping them build some kind of paper mache model out of wet strips of newspaper.

Meanwhile, the kids were anything but stationary. As a very intent little boy walked by them on his way to a center, one of the visitors stopped him to ask about the folders many of the students were holding or consulting.

"This is my Archeology folder," he said confidently, holding it up for the visitor to see. "We all have one, but what's inside of them are different."

"Oh", the visitor said, opening and leafing through it. She leaned over to show the others the handwritten list of questions stapled to the inside cover and neatly organized drawings and "notes" pages stuffed inside.

Looking around the busy room, the visitors pointed out kids reading all kinds of books from formal looking reference books to picture books to poetry anthologies. They noticed two children watching a slide show projected on a wall, and three others sitting around a table in an area labeled "Listening Center", listening intently on headphones while jotting down notes.

One of the visitors pointed to a child reaching up to add sticky notes to a large sheet of chart paper with a timeline drawn on it. Around the room there were more charts with titles like "What we want to know" and "What we found out."

"These kids seem so busy doing different things," one visitor remarked, "but they all seem to know what they are supposed to do!"

And she was right.

When Karen looked up and noticed the visitors, she dried her hands and walked over to greet them.

"Is 'Archeology' a unit from the district's language arts curriculum guide?" one of the visitors asked, referring to the "theme units" meant to provide practice in applying "reading skills" assessed on year-end standardized tests.

"Not really," Karen answered, and then she began to explain that everything the visitors were observing in her reading resource room, including the questions, centers, materials, and information displays.

"Everything we are doing here is aimed at answering a key question that was raised by the students themselves," Karen said, and then she told the story of how it all began.

"One day during recess after lunch, a group of students found some broken pieces of pottery surfacing from the dirt of the school yard," Karen explained. "They became curious about them, collected as many pieces as they could and ran in after lunch to show them to me. Together we brainstormed ideas of what they might be and where they came from. We grew excited at the thought that maybe these were pieces of ancient pottery, or artifacts, left by those who lived here long ago."

Karen told the visitors that the children asked, "Did someone once live here and could there have been a pueblo where our school now stands?"

"Their question," she explained, "became the basis for what we call a 'theme cycle.' This is an extended search for answers to questions posed by the kids themselves. They brainstorm ways to answer their questions and suggest experiences and materials that will help them do that. Of course, I contribute to this myself and guide them along the way."

"My goal is to help them 'learn how to learn' so they can feel competent and confident about their own abilities," she said. "Reading and writing is integrated into the whole process because it is a natural way to learn, record and report what we are discovering. We named this theme cycle 'A Dig in Our Own Backyard' and turned our classroom into a kind of laboratory for archeological exploration."

Karen went on to explain that after they posed the question they decided that the first step was to talk to an expert on the people who once lived here. Karen suggested they needed to talk to an archeologist who could verify and identify the broken pottery and answer some initial questions.

They found an archeology professor at the local university and invited him to their class. Given that he only agreed to meet with 15 of the students, they had to choose representatives who would interview the professor using the questions all of them would brainstorm together. They decided that the interview should be audiotaped so they could all use it later as a resource for their research.

"Excitement grew," Karen said, "when they learned from the interview with the archeologist that they had indeed discovered artifacts from the ruins of an ancient Anasazi Indian pueblo that had once stood on the very site of their school. That discovery led to many more questions."

I recorded these questions and included them in a book, *Whole Language: What's the Difference?* that I later wrote on whole language with two great educators, Carole Edelsky and Barbara Flores. Here's what we wrote:

> Mostly these questions concerned the people who had been there (Where did they come from? Where did they go? How did they live? Did they have gardens? Did they use bows and arrows? Did they dance? What language did they speak? Did they write to each other? Were they happy?) and the pottery they had made (Who made it? Can we make our own? How old is the pottery? What do the designs mean? Why is it on the playground? How was it made? Who made it? Can we make our own?).

Karen organized these questions and many others generated throughout the process into conceptual categories for students to investigate. They gathered resources of varying levels of complexity and set up learning centers to help find answers to their many questions.

As the visitors circulated around the classroom, they observed students at the "Listening Center" probing the taped interview with the archeologist for answers to their questions.

At the "Shard Center", a small group of students were using reference materials to identify the former function of the pottery pieces and the meaning of their designs.

At the "Native American Home Center" three students were studying pictures of pueblo homes that might provide clues to the nature of Anasazi dwellings. "What are you going to do with these pictures?" one of the visitors asked. "We're going to use all these art materials to create our own models of Anasazi houses."

At the "History Center" several students were busily plotting their findings regarding the history of the Anasazi people along a timeline representing the period of 1400-1500. One student explained, "We found out that a long time ago there were 12 other pueblos around here and we're trying to figure out where they were and what happened to them. We're writing our guesses on this bulletin board and then we read stuff to find out if we were right or wrong."

A visitor walked over to two children listening to something on headphones and asked them what it was. They explained that they were listening to recordings of Anasazi chants and poetry that their teacher found in the library, and that they were going to try to make up their own. They wanted to make an Anasazi poetry book for the whole class. In another area, two students were looking over samples of ancient pictographs that were used by the Anasazi. When asked by a visitor why they were studying these pictographs, they replied that they were learning about how the Anasazi wrote and how it is different from the way we write now. They intended to write a story in pictograph writing on one page, and a "translation" of it in their own writing on the next.

Karen told the visitors that some serious questions arose during the time spent investigating this topic. The students wondered if the disappearance of the Anasazi had anything to do with their interaction with Anglo people who began to arrive on this land. Did the Anasazi have difficulties similar to today's pueblo people who experience poverty and other social problems? These kid-posed questions touch on real social, economic and political issues regarding the impact of minority cultures living in the context of a majority culture.

Karen related that some of her students began to wonder about their own histories and identities as Mexican Americans who are often partly of Indian descent. When one of the visitors asked Karen if she tried to avoid these types of "touchy" issues and questions, she replied that she welcomed their investigations of the real world around them and hoped they would continue to do so throughout their lives.

She explained that she believed this was the best way to prepare young people to grow into adults who can solve critical problems that face our society and improve it for everyone.

"Are you sure those were "at risk" kids we observed?" the visitors asked when I escorted them out of Karen's room and back down the hallway.

"Yes" I said, "but they will never know it."

Rick: The Unsinkable Cheerio

Bess has given us such a great example of how reading, writing, speaking, listening, viewing, and performing are central to the whole language classroom. They are all in use and intertwined.

Knowing this, when I was a second grade teacher, class meetings were central to building relationships, creating a safe place to think, and explore the world.

"Some people lie to kids and it's really not fair," Chad stated, one afternoon, as the second graders gathered on the rug in one corner of the classroom to listen to a book and engage in a discussion about it.

The typical flow of the afternoon meeting, which was read first, then discuss, then open the discussion to other things of interest, was interrupted by Chad.

All eyes turned first to Chad and then to me, to see how I'd addressed this condemnation of some unnamed group or individual.

"What do you mean?" I asked.

"I teased my mother to buy this box of cereal because there was a volcano inside it," Chad explained. "The cover of the box had a huge volcano and smoke and fire shooting out and a T-Rex running by. When I got it home it was this tiny piece of plastic."

"It was only this big," Chad said holding up his thumb and forefinger, about two inches apart. "It was dumb," he explained, "because you put some cooking stuff in it and it fizzes a little. There was no fire and smoke."

"Yeah," Lisa chimed in. "They lie to kids. They just want to sell us stuff. Now Chad has to eat that cereal. I know what cereal it is and it's not that good." She looked at Chad and said, "You gotta add a lot of sugar to eat them."

Silence.

The children looked at Chad, Lisa, and again at me, but they were used to the silence I allowed when something important was said.

"We need time to think about things," I'd told them often earlier in the year. Now they knew this to be true. We need time to think and they honored silence.

Theresa finally said, "Let's write them a letter. Let's tell them that they're liars and we know it and we won't buy that cereal ever again."

"I like that cereal," Acacia said. "I'll probably still buy it."

The conversation continued and it was decided that some children in the class would work during writing time that afternoon on a letter to the company. Chad would bring the box and the volcano the next day and we could see the evidence for ourselves. Acacia realized that she could like the cereal, but still agreed that the company misrepresented the free item just to manipulate kids into doing just what Chad had done—teased his mom to get what he wanted (or thought he wanted). The letter was written and sent, but no response arrived.

At a meeting not too long after this, Todd asked, "What about Cheerios? They say that Cheerios are unsinkable, but is that true?" Discussion followed but no conclusion was reached; on my way home from school that day, I purchased a box of Cheerios, some milk, bowls, and spoons.

"Let's find out if Cheerios lies, too," I suggested the next morning. The children were excited and planned out the experiment, with one bowl of Cheerios sitting in the center of our meeting space, milk poured over them, and ready to be observed.

"The bowl is too full," Kenneth suggests. "We need to do it with just one Cheerio."

"Yeah, and we need to hit it with a spoon a few times because they get bonked by the spoon every time you dip it in," Loma recommended.

The class decided that everyone could do this and then, after some discussion, came to the conclusion that everyone would get their own bowl of Cheerios, eat most of them, but leave a few for observation.

They didn't sink. One day later, two days later, and three days later, the lone Cheerios, clearly very soggy, remained afloat. And began to mold.

"Now what?" I asked.

"We need to write to the company and tell them, 'good job,'" Sara began. "If we're writing to tell them they messed up, we need to tell them they've done good, too."

So the class wrote to the company and weeks later received a huge box with Cheerios-letterhead paper, individual boxes of Cheerios, coloring sheets and more.

Prior to the arrival of the box, the children wrote in journals about the volcano and the Cheerios experiment because keeping track of our lives is what literate people do. When the company's products arrived, the joy was palpable and the desire to explore other products began to fill journals at first, and then classroom activity.

Bess and Rick: So What Happened to Whole Language?

The kind of inquiry reflected in these two vignettes is central to whole language classrooms. When we were teaching in the late 1970's, 80's, and early 90's, children were engaged, intense, and studious. Students were serious about increasing their understandings of the highly complex world in which we all live and they were focused on working together to have strong voices that grown-ups would listen to when they expressed their concerns.

Writing was one way to have such a voice and students' growing commitment to being writers was also reflected in their commitment to be informed when they wrote. They were also committed readers and thinkers who were willing to do research, interview people, be tentative, refine conclusions, and inform others about what they had learned.

Children read and wrote, spoke and listened, with the intensity of true learners. That remains a central goal of whole language. What we must recognize is that whole language is joyful, and in addition to what we've shown above, also includes self-selecting and sharing of literature, singing, enjoying poetry, and other authentic literacy experiences that encourage students to fall in love with the act of reading for a lifetime.

If you are a teacher or a parent, you might now be wondering why you've never seen classrooms that look like those in our vignettes. You may be wondering what happened to whole language. To understand the answer to this question we need to view it from a historical perspective.

The whole language movement continued to grow rapidly across school systems and teacher preparation programs throughout the 1980's and 1990's. Spurred by the publication of this book and others, enthusiastic and energized teachers attended national and regional whole language conferences and workshops and even formed local whole language support groups to refine their knowledge and practice. Whole language was well-accepted by professional literacy organizations, and research results were favorable. It seemed like whole language was here to stay.

But then, to the surprise and dismay of the literacy community, ideological, political and corporate powers converged in a concerted effort to discredit whole language and eliminate it from our nation's public schools.

Even while whole language was flourishing, a backlash against it was building. Publishers of commercial reading programs ("basal readers") were becoming alarmed that school districts were no longer purchasing and mandating the use of their products. While some publishers attempted to produce "whole language programs", it was soon apparent that the whole language movement was cutting into their historically huge profits.

When California, which was one of their largest customers, adopted a "literature-based" program that excluded commercial reading programs, the industry took notice. Meanwhile, pushback against whole language was also growing from the religious and conservative right who wanted stricter control (censorship) over reading materials, a return to traditional authoritarian instruction, and an emphasis on isolated phonics instruction.

These forces were already at work when, in 1989, President George H. W. Bush called for comprehensive school reform based upon some federally funded and heavily promoted pro-phonics reports such as *Becoming a Nation of Readers*. The National Business Roundtable (NBRT) representing 200 of the nation's most powerful corporations, including McGraw-Hill, the largest educational publisher of phonics based commercial reading programs, answered the call with an educational agenda that would set the stage for decades of education "reform" policies and legislation.

This agenda for public education prominently featured the goals of curriculum standardization, test-based accountability, and a reward-and-punish policy toward school performance. Although conservative ideology and the thirst for profit were factors at play, the real motive behind the NBRT agenda was to ensure that U.S. corporations would remain competitive in the 21st century global market. They would achieve this by turning schools into "workforce development systems" that would produce future workers with very narrowly defined literacy proficiencies and a predilection for passivity and compliance.

Whole language, with its emphasis on wide reading, critical thinking, and personal and social empowerment, presented a serious obstacle in the path toward producing such domesticated workers. It needed to be eliminated.

Within little more than a decade, across both Republican and Democratic administrations, this corporate agenda for education was encoded into law, first through the *Reading Excellence Act* of

1998, followed by the *No Child Left Behind Act of 2001* (which included *Reading First* mandates), and most recently by the *Race to the Top* initiative instituting the Common Core State Standards and national assessments.

The media played a major role in the attacks on whole language by launching a major disinformation campaign to convince the public that whole language was a failure and that phonics was the panacea for "illiteracy." Later they colluded in spreading the myth that federal control over literacy standards and curriculum would keep the U.S. from falling behind in international standings.

Equally influential were powerful foundations such as the Bill and Melinda Gates Foundation, "think tanks" such as the Heritage and Hoover institutes, federally funded research centers such as the National institute for Child Health and Human Development (NICHD), and influential corporate lobbies such as the American Legislative Exchange Commission (ALEC), all of which paved the way for public acceptance of the corporate coup over literacy education and U.S. public education.

So to understand what happened to whole language and why it was attacked, we need to appreciate that it is the very antithesis of the kind of education that corporate-driven reform policies aim to institute in our nation's public schools. This table summarizes just some of the ways in which whole language stands in direct opposition to corporate-driven policies that currently govern U. S. education.

Whole Language	**Corporate "Reform"**
Self-selected multicultural literature	Prescribed reading material
Teaching for individual strengths & needs	One-size-fits all reading programs

Authentic, teacher based assessment	High stakes standardized testing
Collaborative student-centered curriculum	Standards-based curriculum
Teacher as reflective practitioner	Mandated instruction
Achieving social justice and equity	Achieving global competitiveness

Becoming Political

Over the last two decades, proponents of whole language have learned important lessons regarding the political nature of teaching, learning and literacy. We've also learned that if we want whole language to survive we cannot remain neutral in the struggle for democratic, child-centered schools that honor the language and culture of students and the professionalism of teachers. Although whole language educators face formidable foes, they have not given up and they have not been silent in the face of political power. In fact, whole language teachers are at the forefront of a growing resistance movement to take back our schools and restore teacher professionalism, community voice, and democratic principles to public education.

It is no coincidence that in 2011, whole language educators were among the leaders of the "Save Our Schools March and National Call to Action" that brought thousands of teachers, parents, community activists, as well as prominent educators and public figures, to Washington DC for a mass rally, march and activist conference.

This three-day event had a rippling effect that mobilized a movement to take back our schools that is now sweeping our country, from the streets of Chicago to the barrios of New Mexico. National activist organizations such as Save Our Schools (SOS), United Opt Out (UOO), Network for Public Education (NPE), and the Badass Teachers Association (BATs) are working to end the corporate driven policies that are crippling and closing our public schools and denying our nation's students universal access to an equitable and enriching education.

Members of the AFT and NEA, the major teachers' unions, are applying pressure on their national leaders to stand up against federal policies, and where needed, are forming member based "caucuses" to challenge the local union establishment.

Whole language advocates are no longer alone. Educators, parents and community activists throughout the country have now joined in the struggle to provide a great education to every child.

We have come to realize that in fighting for the survival of whole language theory and practice, we are really fighting for the soul of public education. We believe that Ken Goodman and those who shared his vision of education have known this all along. And while it has been decades since the first publication of this mighty little book, we believe we are finally poised to make Ken's vision a reality. It has never been more relevant, or more important than it is now.

Preface To The 1986 Edition

How whole is whole?

Some of the most effective whole language teachers aren't sure they are whole language teachers. Like all dedicated teachers, they're never quite satisfied with themselves. They continue to do things in their teaching that they think may be inconsistent with "pure" whole language theory. It is not the intention of this book to create a "wholier than thou" view of whole language teaching.

In indicating what's whole about whole language, the characterizations of whole language teachers and the criteria for whole language teaching are those of the author. Whole language is clearly a lot of things to a lot of people; it's not a dogma to be narrowly practiced. It's a way of bringing together a view of language, a view of learning, and a view of people, in particular two special groups of people: kids and teachers. Nothing in this book should discourage any teacher or group of teachers from developing their own version of whole language.

The book's major purpose is to describe the essence of the whole language movement - its basis, its features, and its future. More specifically it will:

- Describe what we know about language and language development.

- Present a whole language perspective on literacy development, both reading and writing.

- Provide criteria that parents and teachers can use in helping children to develop literacy.

- Mention examples of whole language initiatives that are already at work.

- Suggest directions for building whole language initiatives and transforming existing commercial programs into teacher developed whole language "programs".

More than anything else, whole language can be thought of as an educational approach conducted by whole language teachers. Perhaps this book will help them to recognize and define themselves.

1

Whole Language: The Easy Way To Language Development

This riddle has long troubled parents, teachers, and scholars: learning language sometimes seems ridiculously easy and sometimes impossibly hard. And the easy times are outside school, the hard times in school.

Virtually all human babies learn to speak their home language remarkably well in a very short time, without any formal teaching. But when they go to school, many appear to have difficulty, particularly with written language, even though they are instructed by diligent teachers using expensive and carefully developed materials.

We are beginning to work out this seeming paradox. Careful observation is helping us to understand better what makes language easy or hard to learn. Many school traditions seem to have actually hindered language development. In our zeal to make it easy, we've made it hard.

How? Primarily by breaking whole (natural) language up into bite-size, but abstract little pieces. It seemed so logical to think that little children could best learn simple little things. We took apart the language and turned it into words, syllables, and isolated sounds. Unfortunately, we also postponed its natural purpose - the communication of meaning - and turned it into a set of abstractions, unrelated to the needs and experiences of the children we sought to help.

In homes, children learn oral language without having it broken into simple little bits and pieces. They are amazingly good at learning language when they need it to express themselves and understand others, as long as they are surrounded by people who are using language meaningfully and purposefully.

This is what many teachers are learning again from children: keep language whole and involve children in using it functionally and purposefully to meet their own needs. That simple, very basic discovery is leading to some dramatic, exciting changes in schools. Put aside the carefully sequenced basal readers, spelling programs, and handwriting kits. Let the readiness materials, the workbooks, and the ditto masters gather dust on the shelves - or better yet, donate them to community paper drives. Instead, invite pupils to use language. Get them to talk about things they need to understand. Show them it's all right to ask questions and listen to the answers, and then to react or ask more questions. Suggest that they write about what happens to them, so they can come to grips with their experiences and share them with others.

Encourage them to read for information, to cope with the print that surrounds them everywhere, to enjoy a good story.

This way, teachers can work with children in the natural direction of their growth. Language learning then becomes as easy in school as out. And it's more interesting, more stimulating, and more fun for the kids and their teachers. What happens in school supports and expands what happens outside of school. Whole language gets it all together: the language, the culture, the community, the learner, and the teacher.

What makes language very easy or very hard to learn?

It's easy when:	It's hard when:
It's real and natural.	It's artificial.
It's whole.	It's broken into bits and pieces.
It's sensible.	It's nonsense.
It's interesting.	It's dull and uninteresting.
It's relevant.	It's irrelevant to the learner.
It belongs to the learner.	It belongs to somebody else.
It's part of a real event.	It's out of context.
It has social utility.	It has no social value.
It has purpose for the learner.	It has no discernible purpose.
The learner chooses to use it.	It's imposed by someone else.
It's accessible to the learner.	It's inaccessible.
The learner has power to use it.	The learner is powerless.

These lists show that whole language is more pleasant and more fun for both pupils and teachers. Is it also more effective? Yes, it is. With the language they've already learned, children bring to school their natural tendency to want to make sense of the world. When schools break language into bits and pieces, sense becomes nonsense, and it's always hard for kids to make sense out of nonsense. Each abstract bit and piece that is learned is soon forgotten as kids go on to further fractured fragments. In the end, they begin to think of school as a place where nothing ever seems to make sense.

That's why learning language in the real world is easy, and learning language in school should be easy, but is often hard.

What makes language learning hard?

A bottom-up view of learning

Moving from small to large units has an element of adult logic: wholes are composed of parts; learn the parts and you've learned the whole. But the psychology of learning teaches us that we learn from the whole to parts. That's why whole language teachers only deal with language parts - letters, sounds, phrases, sentences - in the context of whole real language.

Artificial skill sequences

Many so-called "skills" were arbitrarily chosen. Whatever research they're based on was done with rats and pigeons - or with children who were treated in the research like rats and pigeons. Rats are not kids; rats don't develop language or think human thoughts. Artificial skill sequences turn schools into mazes for children to stumble through.

Misplaced focus: language for itself

When the purpose of instruction is to teach language for its own sake, or to make kids discuss language like linguists, then the learner is distracted from what he or she is trying to say or understand through language.

Uninteresting, non-meaningful, irrelevant lesson

Uninteresting, irrelevant exercises are particularly tough

on minority children who are constantly being reminded of the distance between their world and the school world. It's hard to motivate kids when the stuff they are asked to read and write, hear and say, has no relation to who they are, what they think, and what they do.

What makes language learning easy?

Relevance

Language should be whole, meaningful, and relevant to the learners.

Purpose

Pupils should use language for their own purposes. Outside school, language functions because users want to say or understand something. In whole language classrooms, the kids own their own language and teachers respect this ownership.

Meaning

Pupils should learn through language while they learn language. Language is learned best when the focus is not on the language but on the meaning being communicated. We learn through language at the same time that we're developing language. We don't learn to read by reading; we learn to read by reading signs, packages, stories, magazines, newspapers, TV guides, billboards.

Respect

Schools should build on the language development children have attained before they start school, and on the experiences they have outside school. Whole language respects the learners: who they are, where they come from, how they talk, what they read, and what experiences they already had before coming to school. That way there are no disadvantaged children as far as the school is concerned. There are only children who have unique backgrounds of language and experience, who have learned to learn from their own experiences, and who will continue to do so if schools recognize who and where they are.

Power

School programs should be seen as part of the empowerment of children. Schools must face the bitter fact that children tend to become literate and succeed in school in proportion to the amount of power to use their literacy they and their families possess. Helping pupils become literate will not in itself give them power if society denies them power. But helping them to achieve a sense of control and ownership over their own use of language and learning in school, over their own reading, writing, speaking, listening, and thinking, will help to give them a sense of their potential power. Schools with effective whole language initiatives can help children to achieve power; they can provide real access to personally and socially useful knowledge through development of thought and language.

2

Language: What And Why?

What would we do without language? We'd still be smart, but terribly frustrated. Language enables us to share our experiences, learn from each other, plan together, and greatly enhance our intellect by linking our minds with others of our kind.

Many people think that if animals could talk - as in the Dr. Doolittle books - they would say intelligent things. Not so, for two reasons. Only humans are able to think symbolically - let systems of meaningless symbols represent our thoughts and through them our experiences, feelings, emotions, and needs. That's what makes human language possible. We also have an intense need for social interaction. That's what makes human language necessary.

Some animals have the ability to produce at least as varied a range of sounds as humans use in speech - mynah birds and parrots, for example. But their sounds lack the symbolic quality of language: they do not represent thought. If we could talk with them, we'd discover that they have nothing to say, that they lack what we have: intellectual capacity and the need for language.

What is language?

Sharing and growing

Language begins as a means of communication between members of the group. Through it, however, each developing child acquires the life view, the cultural perspective, the ways of meaning particular to its own culture. As children master a specific language, they also come to share a specific culture and its values. Language makes it possible to link minds in an incredibly subtle and complex manner.

Language is used to reflect on our own experience and to symbolically express it to ourselves. And through language, we share what we learn with other people. In this way, humanity learns what no one individual person could ever master. Society builds learning upon learning, through language. We even share our aesthetic and emotional responses to experiences. Narratives and poetry can so completely represent the experience of the writer that readers or listeners feel the same emotions as if the actual experience were theirs. In fiction, language can actually create experience.

Written language greatly expands human memory by making it possible to store far more knowledge than any brain is capable of storing. Moreover, written language links us with people in faraway places and distant times, with dead authors. When written language could be cheaply reproduced and widely disseminated, information became a source of power. Limitations on literacy, or on its uses, became limitations on social and personal power.

Social and personal

Language is not a gift given to just a few people. Everyone possesses the gift of developing language, and many of us learn more than one, as the need arises in our lives. But this universality should not mask the unique achievement of each individual in language learning. As babies, we start with a capacity and a need to communicate with others, and we create language for ourselves. In doing that, each one of us moves toward the language of the home and community, but even so, each person's language retains personal characteristics. Each voice is recognizably different; each person's language has a distinctive style, as each person's thumbprint is not quite the same as anyone else's.

Language learning is often thought of as imitation. But people are more than parrots who produce sensible sounding nonsense. Human language represents what the language user is thinking, not simply what other people have said. How else could we express new ideas in response to new experiences? Human language makes it possible to express new ideas and be understood by other people who have never heard such ideas expressed before.

Yet if language were only our own, it would not serve our needs in communicating with others. We must come to share a language with our parents, our families, our neighbors, our people. Remarkably, the personal power to create language is shaped by the social need to understand others and to be understood by them, and the individual's language soon falls within the norms of the language(s) of the community.

Symbolic and systematic

Symbols have no meaning in themselves. "When I use a word," Humpty Dumpty said, in rather a scornful tone, "it means just what I choose it to mean - neither more nor less."

We can combine the symbols - sounds in oral language or letters in written language - into words and let them represent things, feelings, ideas. But what they mean is what we, individually and socially, have decided they will mean. The symbols must be accepted by others if the language is to work for us, but if we need to, we can stretch or modify them to mean new things. Societies and individuals are constantly adding, shifting, or modifying symbols to meet new needs and express new ideas.

But we need more than symbols. We need systems of organizing the symbols so that they represent not just things, feelings, and ideas but dynamic links: how events happen, why they happen, how they affect us, and so on. Language must have *system* as well as symbols, order and rules for producing it, so the same rules can be used for comprehending it.

Of course we can think of language as composed of sounds, letters, words, and sentences. But language cannot be used to communicate unless it is a systematic whole in the context of its use. Language must have symbols, system, and a context of usage.

Grammar is the system of language. It includes the limited number of rules necessary to produce an almost infinite number of utterances that will be understood by speakers of a specific language. Grammar provides word order and inflections (affixes for indicating person, number, tense). That's the most important thing a child learns before school. But the rules can't be learned imitatively since they are never visible in language. Rather, children infer them from experience. By learning to talk and understand speech, children demonstrate their remarkable ability to make these inferences.

Different and changing

There likely never was a human society without oral language.

Prehistoric people, like the primary groups modern people belong to, required immediate, face-to-face communication, and oral language works well for that purpose. But language is not limited to speaking and hearing. We can use any symbol system to create language - or to represent it. Morse code was created to represent language for telegraph and radio use. Ships developed systems of signals using flashing lights or semaphore flags where distances were too great for voice communication. Tactile systems like Braille were developed to give blind people a means of access to print. And visual systems of hand signs were developed by and for deaf people deprived of access to aural communication.

It was not until societies required communication over time and space beyond the reach of the human voice that full forms of written language developed. People came to need to communicate with friends, family or trade partners who did not live nearby. The culture became too complex for oral preservation and transmission. Written language was created to extend the social memory of the community and its communicative reach.

In the contemporary world, language even includes forms for communicating to and through computers and other machines. Whole language curricula accept the responsibility of the school to deal with the whole of language in this sense too.

But since individuals and communities are always changing, so language must change, always adapting to meet the personal and social needs of users. Just think about the following:

- The language of each generation is somewhat different from that of each prior generation. As we get older, we get "set in our ways." Young people are likely to question the *status quo*, and to adopt new language to represent changing lifestyles and life views.

- A certain portion of language comes into quick being among a particular group - musicians, teenagers, scientists, writers, activists - and achieves quick and widespread circulation. Slang appears and disappears. But not all of it is short-lived; sometimes a portion finds its way into more permanent language.

- Special forms of language develop among groups of people who share common interests and experiences: highly technical terminology and/or colorful metaphors. Doctors, lawyers, teachers, computer hackers, CB radio users, to name a few, develop a *jargon* understood only by the initiated. The British term is *registers,* special forms of language for use in special circumstances. We all have registers, in our jobs, our special interests, our religious and political activities.

- All languages are really families of dialects. People separated by distance, by physical barriers like rivers, mountains, or oceans, by social class, racial discrimination, or legal segregation develop variant forms of the language they share, differences in vocabulary, sounds, grammar, and idiom. Changes within each dialect reflect changes in the life experiences of each group and cause the dialects to drift apart, or at least to maintain their distance, even in an age of electronic communication. Schools should welcome the dynamic, fluid nature of language. How marvelous the variety of language, dialects, and registers of pupils! How satisfying for teachers to support the full range of language development rather than confining it to arbitrary "proper" or "standard" language.

Why is language important?

Is language innate? Some scholars think so, especially when they look at how early and how well children learn it. But I think there's a much better explanation of why children achieve such universal precocious control of language.

Language for communication

Children are literally driven to learn language by their *need to communicate*. Sure, human beings are endowed with the ability to think symbolically. But actual language development is a matter of survival. At birth we are totally helpless. We depend for survival on our ability to get the attention of those around us.

People must also communicate to be fully functional human beings. Children have a great deal to learn as they develop, and almost none of it is a simple matter of maturation (though maturation is a factor in much of our learning). They must be in constant intimate communication with other human beings, and language is the key to communication. It is the means by which they come to share the sense that others have made of the world, as they seek to make sense of it for themselves. They learn language because they need it to survive. And they find it easy to learn because the purpose for learning it is clear to them.

Babies are aware of what language does before they are aware of how it does it. Even before they are aware of its communicative potential, they use it for social participation. People around them interact through language - well then, they will too. Very young children already vocalize when they hear other people talking. At six months or so, a child sitting in a high chair at the family dinner table will literally drown out other conversation with its own oral participation, a sure source of enjoyment and good feelings in most families. Often the first notable "words" are social signs like *bye-bye*. Such words don't communicate, but they establish an interpersonal function for language.

Soon children begin to have more explicitly communicative uses for language, to comment on the world or to express a need. Now their language grows rapidly to meet their new needs. They learn language as they use language to learn, and meanwhile they learn about language. From the beginning, all three kinds of language learning are simultaneous in the context of whole speech events.

Language for learning

Language becomes the medium of thought and of learning. In an important way, language development also enters the learning process directly. E.B. Smith suggests that cognitive development has three phases: perceiving, in which the child attends to particular aspects of experience; ideating, in which the child reflects on the experience; and presenting, in which the knowledge is expressed in some way. In this sense, it is not until an idea has been presented that learning is complete.

Language is the most common form of expression. From the earliest preschool learning and throughout life, it is important for people to have opportunities to present what they know, to share it through language, and in the course of this presentation, to complete the learning. This form of language development relates directly to ultimate success in school.

More than one language

Children born into bilingual or multilingual settings come to understand all the languages of their surroundings and to speak the ones they need to. Is it confusing for children to learn more than the language at the same time? No, not normally. They learn to speak to Grandma in her language, to the family in theirs, to the kids on the street in the language of the neighborhood. It has never surprised children in multilingual settings that there was more than one language spoken by the people around them. They simply sort out who speaks and understands what and when, and to whom to use which. Language is easy to learn when it's needed and available.

Many bilingual children fully comprehend a home language, but often respond in English in conversations. These children are showing their sensitivity to the subtle social values and complex functions of each language. They recognize that many of the people around them are bilingual, that each language tends to be used in particular situations by different family members and neighbors of different ages. They apply this sensitivity to meeting their own linguistic needs.

And please, do not believe that bilingual children are disadvantaged in some academic way. They are at a disadvantage only if their linguistic strengths are underappreciated and schools are failing to build on their strengths.

Bilingual children learn more than one language for the same reason that monolingual children learn only one: they learn what they need. That explains why foreign language programs in American schools have been so unsuccessful. The language is isolated from real speech and literacy events, and most American children have no use for the second language as they learn it. To be successful, school second language programs must incorporate authentic functional language opportunities. Canadian immersion schools, where French as a second language is also used as the language of instruction, clearly demonstrate the point.

3

Language Learning: How Does It Happen?

Language is not innate, and not learned as imitation. Nor can human language be learned the way rats learn to run mazes in some simple stimulus- response manner. To control language, one must control the rules of language, and those must be invented and tried out by the learners.

Language learning is a process of social and personal invention. Each person invents language all over again in trying to communicate with the world. But these inventions involve the use of the surrounding public language, and they are constantly tested, modified, abandoned, or perfected in use against it Parents and siblings do not really teach language. They help to shape its development by the way they respond. Fortunately for most babies, family members are so anxious to understand what the infant is saying that the earliest attempts at language are successful out of proportion to their merit. Anything vaguely close to recognizable language used in what appears to be an attempt to accomplish a linguistic function will tend to work. When it doesn't, the response may suggest another way to accomplish the goal, even if it's only vaguely understood.

All learning involves risk. Families tend to cherish first attempts at language and therefore diminish the risk to learners. They are free to fail and try again. Schools need to be equally encouraging of risk-taking in language development.

Halliday suggests that children often initiate language and parents follow along behind, tracking, responding, but letting the children set the pace and be in charge of their own development. There is so much language in the experience of young children, so much opportunity for testing out rules and hypotheses, using interchanges with others as resource material, that in due time control over the rules of the language is established, as well as over the sound system and the vocabulary. In the same way children gain control over the subtle pragmatic constraints on language, differentiating play from serious communication, becoming aware of who may say what to whom and when.

Function before form.

Form follows function in language development, as in so many things. Children know what they want to do with language, and that stimulates their drive to control the form of language so that it meets their needs. It's worth repeating: language is easy to learn if it meets a functional need the child feels.

But here's where conventional wisdom gets in the way of understanding. Do you have to have control of sounds before you speak, of phonics before you read, of spelling before you write, of vocabulary before you use language? Not really. Children talk comprehensibly before they control many of the sounds of the adult dialect. They produce sentences long before they control the rules of sentence making. If they had to wait to control conventional spelling, they would never write, or even discover why spelling is important. Language use begins with a function and then involves experimenting with the language forms necessary to fulfill that function. Of course errors are made in the forms as they develop. We relish babies making them. But we become less tolerant of the miscues of older children, and somehow begin to think that development can go from stage to stage error-free. Whole language accepts the reality of learning through risk-taking and error. Scribbling, reversed letters, invented spellings, creative punctuation, and reading and writing miscues are charming indications of growth toward control of the language processes. Kids are universally able to sort out language as they use it to meet their functional needs. If their language use in school is authentic, then they will not find it hard to get control of the language forms they need.

Whole to part

Baby books all have places to record a child's first word. But the idea that children begin with words and then put them together to make sentences is only an illusion. The illusion arises because physical control over the articulation of sound sequences is limited at first. But each *da-da* or *ma-ma* really is a whole utterance that means something like "Hey, come and get me. I want some attention." Children go through what some scholars have called a holophrastic stage. Each "word" is really an undifferentiated glob of language with a generalized meaning in certain situational contexts. As language develops, the glob begins to be differentiated into words and word parts. It takes on a grammatical structure, and at the same time moves toward more definite and specific meanings near to, but not necessarily the same as, the adult meanings. The child's "pick up" may mean both "pick me up" and "put me down".

Language is actually learned from whole to part. We first use whole utterances in familiar situations. Then later we see and develop parts, and begin to experiment with their relationship to each other and to the meaning of the whole. The whole is always more than the sum of the parts and the value of any part can only be learned within the whole utterance in a real speech event.

The rules for producing language utterances are induced from the early holophrastic units. "I taked it." "I pick-upped my toys." "He gots more." "Me wanna turn." So often the errors children make are the best indicators of their growth. When they start to generate their own rules and reveal them, we learn much about them, especially that they feel free to experiment and learn. Keeping children from making mistakes is a sure way to make them insecure and to inhibit their ultimate development.

But whether we're talking about learning to make sense of print as beginning readers, learning to read a TV guide, or learning to write a research report in a high school science class, the constituent parts or "skills" can't be learned outside of the whole experience at any stage of development. You can't learn to write a letter by first learning to write salutations and then opening paragraphs and then formal closings. None of these make any real sense outside a real situation in which a letter is the most useful way of meeting the need to communicate - to get information, to say thanks, to invite some real person to a real event. If we want to keep language learning easy, we have to help learners learn from whole to part.

Learning how to mean

Halliday explains the inseparable relationship between meaning and language development:

The child is learning to be and to do, to act and to interact in meaningful ways. He is learning a system of meaningful behavior; in other words, he is learning a semiotic system. Part of his meaningful action is linguistic. But none of it takes place in isolation; it is always within some social context. So the content of the utterance is the meaning that it has with respect to a given function, to one or other of the things that the child is making language do for him. It is a semiotic act which is interpretable by reference to the total range of semiotic options, the total meaning potential that the child has accessible to him at that moment.

Schools frequently isolate language from its meaningful functional use. Then they change language into non-language. Only in the social context of language usage does it have a meaning potential for the learner, and only in such context is it language and easy to learn. From the very earliest beginnings, language is inseparably related in the child's mind to sensibility. If we turn it into nonsense, then it is not easy to learn but hard.

Speech and literacy events

Oral language occurs in speech events. A speech event includes not only the language text (the connected discourse itself) but also the people speaking and/ or listening, their purposes, intentions, and social relationships. It includes the context of the situation - the physical setting, the cultural and social constraints, the emotions of the participants. The choice of register will depend on all these characteristics of the speech event. Participants in speech events know whether they have been successful in their intentions and modify their participation - including their language - to become more effective.

Written language occurs in literacy events. These have all the characteristics of speech events with one exception. In speech events, both speaker and listener are present, often switching roles. In most literacy events only the writer or the reader is present. The writer must have a *sense* of the audience, the reader a *sense* of the author. Though there is always a situational context of some sort, literacy events usually do not have the close relationship to a physical context that speech events do. So written texts must also include cues that provide those "senses".

More than once we have described how children develop their own language within speech events. They also begin to develop their competence with print in response to literacy events long before they go to school. At a very young age, children respond to books and to print in the environment and to adults reading to them. Optimal literacy development will occur in rich written (printed) language contexts.

Carol Edelsky says schools break the link between authentic language and natural speech and literacy events. They turn language into abstraction and essentially destroy it. This decontextualizing makes it hard to learn language. You will not be surprised to learn that a successful whole language program consists, to the fullest extent possible, of authentic speech and literacy events.

Two forces - outward and inward bound

Physicists talk about the centrifugal force, which causes something to move away from the center (as a ball on a string does when it's being whirled and the whirler lets go of the string), and about the opposing centripetal force (for example, gravity), which causes an object to seek the center. Placing a satellite in orbit is a matter of bringing these forces into balance.

Here is an apt metaphor for the forces shaping children's language. The creative force inside them causes them to invent language and to constantly expand its limits and use. Outside them, the community pushes its language back toward the center of shared language and shared meaning. If the creative forces were unchecked, the individual's language would not work for social communication. But children's need to understand and be understood causes them to be sensitive to social response and to move toward the language norms of the social dialect. Again, it is only when children attempt purposeful use of language in real social contexts that these forces play against each other and shape language. Schools can support this process, but they can't short-circuit it by teaching the social norms in some prior, decontextualized way.

Language in school and out

A simple principle should now be clear. Language development is really the same in and out of school. Whatever makes language easy to learn outside of school will also make it easier to learn in school. And what makes it hard to learn is the same, in school or out. Successful school programs are based on an understanding of natural language development. The school facilitates language if the approach involves authentic speech and literacy events, if the teacher is knowledgeable about language development and able to monitor and support its growth.

Of course there are unique language functions in school that relate to its own character as a community of learners, and to its focus on increasingly advanced and abstract areas of human knowledge. Schools have their unique speech and literacy events. Still, the basic principles of human language learning hold. Language development and learning through language will prosper when schools focus on what makes language easy to learn. This is a theme that will be pursued as we talk about a whole language curriculum in the next chapter.

Is written language different?

Oral and written language are two parallel language processes, different sets of language registers, which overlap to some extent. If you are literate, that means that sometimes writing is a better way of achieving a particular purpose, sometimes talking. You could write your sister who lives in another city, or telephone her. The latter method is more expensive, and doesn't leave a permanent record.

Written language has all the basic characteristics of oral language: symbols and system used in the context of meaningful language acts (literacy events). It is tempting (and people have done it) to treat written language not so much as language itself, but as a kind of coded representation of speech. This is unfortunate for a number of reasons. It leads us, in school, to expect reading and writing to be learned differently from speaking and listening, and to accept the belief that many children will have difficulty becoming literate.

Most people learn to talk before they learn to read and write, and it helps to do so. But hearing-impaired people can learn to read and write. And in learning second languages, many people have more need and opportunity to read than to speak. In this case, reading will often be the first of the four language processes to develop. Simply put, people will learn whatever language forms and processes they need the most.

Written language is not simply a way of recording oral language. For example, consider a simple chart, say a TV or a radio schedule in your newspaper. Because writing uses two-dimensional space, a lot of information can be presented in tabular form. Furthermore, a particular portion of the information can be accessed easily: what's on at 7 p.m., for example.

Functions of written language

Written language has several important functions in a literate society:

- *Environmental print* provides information such as street names, addresses, store names, directions, and regulations (like *Keep off the Grass* or *Curb Your Dog*).

- *Occupational print* is the reading and writing that is part of doing one's job. School age children are students by occupation, but they also use written language as they play at adult occupations.

- *Informational print* is used to store, organize, and retrieve information. It can be very compact and dense, as in the case of phone books, or attractively organized to highlight certain information, as in newspaper advertisements.

- *Recreational print* is the reading and writing we choose to do during our leisure time: fiction and non-fiction material related to hobbies and special interests.

- *Ritualistic print* is the written language many religions use in their rituals. Often texts are in an ancient language not well understood even by the participants.

Learning written language

Why do people create and learn written language? They need it! How do they learn it? The same way they learn oral language, by using it in authentic literacy events that meet their needs. Often children have trouble learning written language in school.

It's not because it's harder than learning oral language, or learned differently. It's because we've made it hard by trying to make it easy. Frank Smith wrote an article called "12 Easy Ways to Make Learning to Read Hard." Every way was designed to make the task easy by breaking it up in small bits. But by isolating print from its functional use, by teaching skills out of context and focusing on written language as an end in itself, we made the task harder, impossible for some children. The one "hard" way Smith advocates is to find out what children are doing and to help them do it. What they are doing is trying to make sense of print. The way to help them do it is to make school a literate environment full of literacy events, with an insightful teacher present to monitor their development toward literacy and help it happen.

4

School: A Whole Language View

These days many people are skeptical about positive, humanistic approaches to teaching and learning that do *not* depend heavily on technology. Technocrats think that education can be packaged in kits, workbooks, and mastery learning programs, and judged by pre-tests and post-tests. They think that whole language teachers don't know what they're doing or what kids are learning. Whole language teachers are accused of thinking they can make kids literate just by loving them.

Whole language teachers need not be defensive or apologetic. They believe in kids, respect them as learners, cherish them in all their diversity, and treat them with love and dignity. That's a lot better than regarding children as empty pots that need filling, as blobs of clay that need molding, or worse, as evil little troublemakers forever battling teachers. Whole language teachers believe that schools exist for kids, not that kids are to be filled and molded by behavior modification or assertive discipline into look-alike, act-alike, talk-alike Barbie and Ken dolls.

Whole language teachers believe there is something special about human learning and human language. They believe all children have language and the ability to learn language, and they reject negative, elitist, racist views of linguistic purity that would limit children to arbitrary "proper" language. Instead, they view their role as helping children to expand on the marvelous language they already use. They expect them to learn and they are there to help them do it Can school be fun? You bet! It not only can be, it should be. Learning in school should be as easy and as much fun as it is outside of school. What's more, if kids are enthusiastic and enjoy learning, then teaching is fun too! Whole language teachers admit they love teaching - and what's wrong with that, even if the pay isn't so great? Whole language teachers are proud professionals!

But there is more to whole language than this positive view of kids, a *whole* lot more, if you'll pardon the pun. Whole language teachers draw on scientific theories rooted soundly in research from linguistics, language development, sociolinguistics, psycholinguistics, anthropology, and education as they build curriculum, plan instruction, evaluate progress. The humanistic and scientific bases of whole language teaching support each other. They make it possible for teachers to operate as effective, compassionate professionals with the type of confidence that's based on knowledge and commitment. In this chapter we'll explore this a bit further.

What is the basis of whole language teaching?

Whole language is firmly supported by four humanistic-scientific pillars. It has a strong theory of learning, a theory of language, a basic view of teaching and the role of teachers, and a language-centered view of curriculum.

A learning theory

Chapter two already spelled it out:

- Language learning is easy when it's whole, real, and relevant; when it makes sense and is functional; when it's encountered in the context of its use; when the learner chooses to use it.

- Language is both personal and social. It's driven from inside by the need to communicate and shaped from the outside toward the norms of the society. Kids are so good at learning language that they can even overcome counter-productive commercial programs.

- Language is learned as pupils learn through language and about language, all simultaneously in the context of authentic speech and literacy events. There is no sequence of skills in language development. Teaching kids about language will not facilitate their use of language. The notion that "first you learn to read and then you read to learn" is wrong. Both happen at the same time and support each other.

- Language development is empowering: the learner "owns" the process, makes the decisions about when to use it, what for and with what results. Literacy is empowering too, if the learner is in control of what's done with it.

- Language learning is learning how to mean: how to make sense of the world in the context of how our parents, families, and cultures make sense of it. Cognitive and linguistic development are totally interdependent: thought depends on language and language depends on thought.

- In a word, language development is a holistic personal-social achievement.

A language theory

Whole language teaching is also based on scientific knowledge and theories about language. Halliday says we have treated language too solemnly but not seriously enough. We have tended to accept stuffy, narrow views of language. Language purists worry us about being totally proper in our language use, and they appoint themselves as judges. This uptight solemnity masks a total lack of respect for human language. It confuses the effectiveness of language with the status of the people who speak it. The language of people with power and social status is taken to be better than the language of people without it. Social attitudes toward language reflect social attitudes toward people.

Ours is a more serious and scientific view of language. Whole language teachers understand that there is no language without symbols and system. Every dialect of every language has register and grammar. People who speak differently are not deficient in any linguistic sense. Mark Twain, with a writer's insight, expressed this well in his explanatory note immediately preceding *Huckleberry Finn*:

> In this book a number of dialects are used, to wit the Missouri Negro dialect; the extremist form of the backwoods South-Western dialect; the ordinary Pike-County dialect; and four modified varieties of this last. The shadings have not been done in a haphazard fashion, or by guess-work; but painstakingly, and with the trustworthy guidance and support of personal familiarity with these several forms of speech.
>
> I make this explanation for the reason that without it many readers would suppose these characters were trying to talk

alike and not succeeding.

Whole language is whole. It does not exclude some languages, some dialects, or some registers because their speakers lack status in a particular society. Every language form constitutes a precious linguistic resource for its users. This does not mean that whole language teachers are not aware of the social values assigned to different language varieties and how these affect people who use them. But they can put these social values in proper perspective.

Language is inclusive, and it is indivisible. Whole language teaching recognizes that words, sounds, letters, phrases, clauses, sentences, and paragraphs are like the molecules, atoms, and subatomic particles of things. Their characteristics can be studied, but the whole is always more than the sum of the parts. If you reduce a wooden table to the elements which compose it, it's no longer a table. The characteristics of carbon, hydrogen, and some other bits may be studied and so help us understand how a table can be, but we don't build a table with them.

Language is language only when it's whole. Whole text, connected discourse in the context of some speech or literacy event, is really the minimal functional unit, the barest whole that makes sense. When teachers and pupils look at words, phrases, sentences, they do so always in the context of whole, real language texts that are part of real language experiences of children.

It had to come. Linguists and others are turning their attention from smaller bits and pieces to whole texts. They have begun to provide information on what makes a text a text and how people are able to produce comprehensible texts and make sense of them. Now we are beginning to realize that we've made mistakes in school when we tried to simplify language learning. Controlled vocabulary, phonic principles, or short, choppy sentences in primers and pre-primers produced non-texts. What we gave children didn't hang together, was unpredictable, and violated the expectations of even young readers who knew already how a real story works. Above it all hung the dark cloud of irrelevance and dullness. And we taught writing by drilling pupils on handwriting, spelling, and other mechanics, and so distracted them from what they already knew through oral language about producing whole functional texts.

Writing and reading are both dynamic, constructive processes. Writers must decide how much to provide so that readers will be able to infer and recreate what the writer created in the first place. Readers will bring to bear their knowledge of the text, their own values, their own experiences, as they make sense of a writer's text. Texts must be real, and not thrown together to fit some vocabulary list or phonics sequence. Writers must have a sense of audience, and readers must have a sense of the writer. Real writers have something to say, and real readers know how to understand and respond.

Whole language teachers have a basic sense of how language works. Lewis Carroll said, "Take care of the sense and the sounds will take care of themselves." Whole language teachers know, when they work with language that is whole and sensible, that all the parts will be in proper perspective and learning will be easy.

A view of teaching

Respect for and understanding of learning and language is matched by respect for and understanding of teaching.

Whole language teachers regard themselves as professionals. They draw constantly on a scientific body of knowledge in carrying out their work; they know about language, learning, kids, curriculum, and methodology. They take responsibility for their successes and failures. And they expect to be given the room to use their professional abilities and knowledge. They expect respect from their pupils, their administrators, and the public, and understand that respect must be earned by professional conduct. They take pride and pleasure in their work. They are confident in their teaching and in their decision-making because they are confident in the humanistic-scientific bases of their practice. They expect a degree of autonomy in their classrooms, for no professional can function if locked into rigid administratively imposed strictures - in their case, commercial programs, curricula, and materials. They vary the use of adopted texts and prescribed curricula to meet the needs of their pupils in accordance with their best professional judgment. They apply criteria to methods, materials, and curricula and evaluate their potential effect on their pupils. In some circumstances they may find it necessary to reject certain commercial prescriptive materials and programs, just as a medical doctor reserves the professional right to reject certain treatments, drugs, and procedures.

Let's not beat around the bush. Basal readers, workbooks, skills sequences, and practice materials that fragment the process are unacceptable to whole language teachers. Their presentation of language phenomena is unscientific, and they steal teachers' and learners' time away from productive reading and writing. Many whole language teachers don't use basals at all, but build their reading and writing curricula practices around children's literature, often in thematic units. Some teachers salvage what they can - whatever good children's literature there is in their basals - to support the whole language initiatives and practices. But some commercial programs - among them so-called mastery-learning programs - are so rigidly based on arbitrary skill drills and rigid pre-test, test, post-test sequences that the program is at odds with whole language criteria. Furthermore, rigid commercial programs monopolize school time and turn progress into progress-through-the-program, rather than progress in real learning. Teachers are reduced to robots: technicians acting out someone else's script. In fact, such tightly controlled commercial programs are often based on assumptions of teacher incompetence. Whole language teachers have the right and obligation to reject them, on behalf of the kids they teach and the professionalism they embody.

Whole language teachers understand that learning ultimately takes place one child at a time. They seek to create appropriate social settings and interactions, and to influence the rate and direction of personal learning. They are utterly convinced that teachers guide, support, monitor, encourage, and facilitate learning, but do not control it. They are aware of the universals of human learning, of language and cognitive processes, but they understand the different paths each learner must take. They expect and plan for growth and do not impose arbitrary standards of performance.

Whole language teachers are never completely satisfied. They keep trying to make the curriculum more relevant, to make language experiences in school as authentic and relevant as those outside school, to reach all children and help them expand their language competence as they continue to learn through language.

A view of curriculum

Integration

If language is learned best and easiest when it is whole and in natural context, then integration is a key principle for language development and learning through language. In fact, language development and content become a dual curriculum. For learners it's a single curriculum focusing on what is being learned, what language is being used for. But for teachers there is always a double agenda: to maximize opportunities for pupils to engage in authentic speech and literacy events while they study their community, do a literature unit on Lloyd Alexander, carry out a scientific study of mice, or develop a sense of fractions and decimals. The teacher evaluates both linguistic and cognitive development. Speaking, listening, writing, and reading are all happening in context of the exploration of the world of things, events, ideas, and experiences. The content curriculum draws on the interests and experiences children have outside of school, and thus incorporates the full range of oral and written language functions. It becomes a broad, rich curriculum that starts where learners are in language and knowledge and builds outward from there.

Individual growth, not achievement of absolute levels, is the goal. Whole language teachers accept pupil differences. They plan for expansion of effectiveness and efficiency in language, and expansion of knowledge and understanding of the world in each individual child.

Language processes are integrated as well. Children speak, listen, write, or read as they need to. If a puppet show is developed to dramatize a Lloyd Alexander story, then the story will be *read*, an outline or script will be *written*, and various class members will participate as *actors*, stage hands, or *audience*. If mice are studied, groups may *discuss* and plan their study, resource materials may be *read*, posters planned and *written*, observations made and *recorded*, *written* and *oral* reports made. Manipulatives in math may be used to explore fractions, findings *discussed*, and conclusions *written-up*. None of this is new, of course. But integration becomes the central motif in a whole language curriculum.

Choice, ownership, relevance

Authenticity is essential. Kids need to feel that what they are doing through language they have chosen to do because it is useful, or interesting, or fun for them. They need to own the processes they use: to feel that the activities are their own, not just school work or stuff to please the teacher. What they do ought to matter to them personally. Achieving the goal of providing for choice, ownership, and relevance throughout the curriculum is neither simple nor easy. But whole language teachers keep these goals in mind to ensure that the curriculum is most effective.

Language across the curriculum

In elementary classrooms with one teacher, this kind of curriculum is not hard to achieve. For departmentalized secondary schools the concept of *language across the curriculum* has spread from England to most other English- speaking countries. Content area teachers are urged to consider how language is used in their fields and then think of their curriculum as a dual curriculum with the double agenda it implies. Math teachers need to think of the language of math as a special register, and to help students learn to control it as they deal with math concepts and the solution of math problems. English teachers, librarians, and specialists in reading and writing need to plan with and even team-teach with content area teachers to achieve greater integration and greater authenticity.

Thematic units

Whole language teachers organize the whole of or a large part of the curriculum around topics or themes: *What are the risks of nuclear war? Is water pollution a danger in our community? The history of our neighborhood. How to take care of hamsters. Nutrition in mice.* They can be science units, social science units/literature units, or units that integrate all three, as well as the arts, humanities, and even physical education. A unit provides a focal point for inquiry, for use of language, for cognitive development. It involves pupils in planning, and gives them choices of authentic, relevant activities within productive studies.

What is a whole language classroom?

The splendid organization of whole language classrooms is not always apparent to a casual observer. The kids and teacher plan together what they will do, when they will do it and how, what materials will be needed, how they will be obtained or distributed, who will be where. Long-range plans provide a general framework, and short-range plans make details explicit. Just listen for the buzz of activity, see the level of participation of kids and teacher, enjoy the sense of well-being and ease everyone exhibits, admire the relatively smooth transitions, and relish the pervasive sense of order. The whole language teacher is clearly in charge, but it may take a visitor a few minutes to locate the busy adult doing many things in many parts of the room.

Clearly some classrooms lend themselves better physically to the range of activities that go on in a whole language classroom than others do. It doesn't help if there are rows of seats bolted to the floor. On the other hand, Lillian Weber has helped New York teachers to conduct open education by literally making use of the school corridors. The view of language, learning, teaching, and curriculum is what makes a whole language classroom; the physical environment can be adapted to fit.

A literate environment

In a whole language classroom, there are books, magazines, newspapers, directories, signs, packages, labels, posters, and every other kind of appropriate print all around. Pupils bring in all kinds of written language materials appropriate to their interests and the curriculum. Primary classrooms have mailboxes, writing centers complete with a wide range of paper and implements, a library comer, a newsstand, and appropriate labels for everything. No one is too young to participate in the creation of a literate environment to dictate a story, label, put together the displays and bulletin boards, or simply experience how the literate environment is created.

Centers and resources

Learning centers are quite common now. Whole language teachers prefer centers organized around topics and thematic units, structured to facilitate the integration of all the language processes with conceptual learning. Specific writing centers or book centers are therefore equipped to facilitate ongoing units as well as general topics. In some skills-oriented programs, centers are places pupils go to do worksheets and skills exercises. That's why it's important for centers in whole language classrooms to be integrated and keyed to the ongoing whole language initiative.

Usually pupils organize their own distribution system. The whole language classroom is theirs, and if given an opportunity, they will ensure that materials are easily available and respected. They will set rules for getting and using materials and equipment, for moving around the room (and out of it). As always, the teacher is omnipresent, watching, mixing in, making sure that the whole language curriculum is not inhibited or blocked, and helping to settle disputes and uncertainties. But a pupil does not need special permission to check for spelling in a dictionary or another book. A small group decides for itself who should get a library book. A pupil asks a classmate to try out a phrase for the story she is writing, and does it without disturbing others.

Whole language materials

Basal readers, sequenced skill programs, or the usual types of commercial instructional materials are really not needed. In fact, workbooks and duplicated skill exercises are inappropriate in whole language classrooms. What is appropriate is anything the children need or want to read or write. Lots of recreational books are needed, fiction and non-fiction, with a wide range of difficulty and interest, and resource materials of all kinds, some particularly prepared for use in school (like beginners' dictionaries and encyclopedias) and some "real world" resources (like phone books, TV guides, and adult reference books).

The money spent on reading, writing, spelling, and handwriting texts *can* be used to keep the classroom supplied with a rich range of authentic resources. Every classroom at every level needs a classroom library, augmented by book clubs and book exchanges, by groups of books borrowed from the public library, by short-term collections from the school library, and by student-authored books produced in the class publishing center. It's very important to have a wide range of books and other materials within immediate reach.

5

Whole Language: What Makes It Whole?

Before we get to specifics, let's consider what distinguishes whole language approaches from other reading-writing methods. Most of the discussion will center on reading, simply because there has been so little teaching of writing, particularly in elementary schools. Perhaps no one could figure out how to make a basal writing series! So we have limited ourselves to isolated spelling and handwriting instruction. It should be said, however, that considerable writing in a holistic way is beginning to be done in elementary schools, mainly because of Donald Graves and his colleagues.

What is not whole language?

Teaching practices, commercial reading programs, and curricula in schools vary widely at the moment, and many of them are simply incompatible with whole language instruction. Whole language firmly rejects such things as these:

- Isolating skill sequences.

- Slicing up reading and writing into grade slices, each slice neatly following and dependent on prior ones.

- Simplifying texts by controlling their sentence structures and vocabulary, or organizing them around phonic pattern.

- Equating reading and writing with scores on tests of "sub-skills".

- Isolating reading and writing instruction from its use in learning, or in actual reading and writing.

- Believing there are substantial numbers of learners who have difficulty learning to read or write for any physical or intellectual reason.

Skills-technology views

Contemporary reading instruction has been dominated by several key factors:

The development of a technology of reading instruction

This technology grew between 1920 and 1960. Linguists, psycholinguists, and sociolinguists were busy elsewhere, and North American educators and researchers put great faith in technology. Behavioral psychology strongly dominated. The technology incorporated narrow views of language and language learning.

Tests: the focus of the technology

Standardized reading tests assume that reading can be

subdivided neatly into sub-skills that can easily be sequenced and measured. Learning to read means scoring better on tests of these sequenced bits and pieces: letter-sound relationships, isolated words, abstract definitions, fractured sentences, and paragraphs pulled out of the middle of longer coherent texts. With faith in technology, teachers, school boards, and legislators came to rely more and more on tests. At their worst, tests decide promotion or failure, admission to special programs and ability tracks, and the effectiveness of teachers. In extreme cases, they have even become the curriculum. This very abusive use of tests has driven teachers to seek alternatives that are more positive, more humane and fairer to learners, more soundly based on modern research and theory, and more effective in producing learning. Teachers know they know more about their pupils than the tests can show them.

Basal readers in every classroom up to grade 8

Basals, basals, everywhere! Basals vary somewhat in the criteria used to organize and sequence them, but essentially they are organized around controlled vocabulary. So, learning to read becomes learning to recognize words: the most common words appear in primers and early books, while less common words are introduced gradually over the years; behavioral psychology is used to develop rules for how often a word must be repeated in a text once it is introduced, and how many words should be introduced per page; separate basals are created for each grade.

A view of words as the key units in learning to read and write

There have been noisy public battles between those advocating explicit phonics approaches and those advocating teaching words as wholes. The latter use a range of ways to "attack" words in order to learn them, including phonics. The former argue that once kids know "the sounds of the letters" they can read and don't need anything else. But both agree that learning to read is a matter of learning words. In fairness, it should be said that whole-word advocates tend to be more concerned with giving kids good stories. There are even some who have tried to combine a strong explicit phonics program with having the pupils read real stories.

Direct instruction for reading

The technology has produced workbooks, ditto masters, extra practice for learners who get low test scores, and supplementary "enrichment" materials for the high scorers. Strangely, the huge allocation of time for reading instruction does not mean that a lot of time is spent on actual reading. Little time is left after skills drill exercises, phonics drills, and workbook exercises with nothing longer than a line or two. Writing gets even less time, as does oral language, science, social studies, humanities, arts, or thinking about real problems.

Severely labeled children

Readers are labeled remedial, disabled, or dyslexic if they don't do well in tests and technologized reading programs. They then get more isolated drills on phonics and word attacks, and even less time for learning language while using language to learn. What they suffer from most is the fact of being labeled.

Dislike of reading

Large numbers have managed to survive the technology and learn to read and write with at least moderate effectiveness, but in the process have learned to think of reading and writing as unpleasant activities to be done only when absolutely necessary. They can read and write, but they usually choose not to do so if the choice is their own to make.

Breaking some icons

There are some aspects of the reading technology that have become so firmly entrenched in conventional reading instruction that they need special attention to indicate why they have no place in whole language classrooms.

Readiness

Some good reasons lay behind special readiness programs. Children need time to mature; rushing them is counter-productive. So when Washburne said that a mental age of 6 was necessary for success in learning to read, many people eagerly accepted that, though even at the time questions were raised about the validity of the research. Similarly, people could see that when children start school they haven't yet developed fine muscle control, so they should perhaps not be expected to write with adult pencils and pens. Unfortunately, bad reasoning combined these facts with a lack of understanding of human language development and use. What resulted were non-language activities and abstractions that had nothing to do with children's readiness for written language development.

Real readiness is intrinsic when language is real. Good kid-watchers know when children see a need for reading and writing, have confidence in themselves, and want to join "the literacy club." Whole language teachers don't rush children, but neither do they distract them from natural functional language use and development. They simply support them as they build on what they already know.

Phonics

Phonics is the set of relationships between the sound system of oral language and the letter system of written language. Phonics methods of teaching reading and writing reduce both to matching letters with sounds. It is a flat-earth view of the world, since it rejects modem science about reading and writing and how they develop. Phonics programs tend to be unscientific even in their presentation of phonic relationships. It simply isn't true that "when two vowels go walking, the first does the talking" except in a limited number of cases, which must be already known to the reader in order for the rule to be sensible.

Besides, English vowels don't just come in long and short varieties. The difference in the vowels in the following list of words will vary from dialect to dialect: *frog, fog, bog, dog, smog, cog, hog, jog*. But not one of the sounds is a "long o." Phonics programs can't deal with dialect differences unless they acknowledge that each dialect has a different set of phonics rules. Moreover, phonics methods ignore normal shifts in pronunciation that happen as words add affixes. Notice the letter "t" in *site, situate, situation*. The "t" stays in each word even though the sound shifts as the affixes are added. That's good, because it preserves the meaning relationship between these related words.

But even a more scientific phonics approach would be insufficient as a method for teaching reading and writing. The logic of phonics instruction is that letters can be coded as sounds, or sounds as letters. Then these can be blended to produce reading or writing. But that doesn't produce meaningful language - it only produces strings of sounds or letters.

Instead, children discover the alphabetic principle when they learn to write. There are relationships between letter patterns and sound patterns. They do what they do in all language learning: they search for rules. That leads to invented spelling. But spelling is standardized in English (and most other languages), so the rules produce only a possible spelling, not necessarily the standard one. Thus children learn to keep their eyes open for standard spellings as they read, and to suspend the rules when they don't work. Gradually they move toward conventional spelling in their writing.

Readers are seeking meaning, not sounds or words. They may use their developing phonics generalizations to help when the going gets tough. If they are lucky enough not to have been taught phonics in isolation, with each letter equally important, then they will not be diverted from developing the strategies necessary to select just enough graphic information to get to the sense they are seeking.

In whole language classrooms readers and writers develop control over the phonic generalizations in the context of using written language sensibly. These self-developed rules are not over-learned and artificial as they would be if they were imposed by a structured reading and spelling program. Whole language teachers do not ignore phonics. Rather they keep phonics in the context of real reading and real writing.

What are the principles of whole language?

Whole language is an attempt to get back to basics in the real sense of that word - to set aside basals, workbooks, and tests, and to return to inviting kids to learn to read and write by reading and writing real stuff.

Principles for reading and writing

- Readers construct meaning during reading. They use their prior learning and experience to make sense of the texts.

- Readers predict, select, confirm, and self-correct as they seek to make sense of print. In other words, they guess or make hypotheses about what will occur in the text. Then they monitor their own reading to see whether they guessed right or need to correct themselves to keep making sense. Effective reading makes sense. Efficient reading does it with the least amount of effort and input. Rapid readers tend to have high comprehension because they are both effective and efficient.

- Writers include enough information and detail so what they write will be comprehensible to their readers. Effective writing makes sense for the intended audience. Efficient writing includes only enough for it to be comprehensible.

- Three language systems interact in written language: the grapho-phonic (sound and letter patterns), the syntactic (sentence patterns), and the semantics (meanings). We can study how each one works in reading and writing, but they can't be isolated for instruction without creating non-language abstractions. All three systems operate in a pragmatic context, the practical situation in which the reading and writing is taking place. That context also contributes to the success or failure of the reading or writing.

- Comprehension of meaning is always the goal of readers.

- Expression of meaning is always what writers are trying to achieve.

- Writers and readers are strongly limited by what they already know, writers in composing, readers in comprehending.

Principles for teaching and learning

- School literacy programs must build on existing learning and utilize intrinsic motivations. Literacy is an extension of natural whole language learning: it is functional, real, and relevant.

- Literacy develops from whole to part, from vague to precise, from gross to fine, from highly concrete and contextualized to more abstract, from familiar contexts to unfamiliar.

- Expression (writing) and comprehension (reading) strategies are built during functional, meaningful, relevant language use.

- Development of the ability to control the form of reading and writing follows, and is motivated by, the development of the functions for reading and writing.

- There is no hierarchy of sub-skills, and no necessary universal sequence.

- Literacy develops in response to personal/ social needs. Children growing up in literate environments become literate before they come to school. There is no one-to-one correspondence between teaching and learning. The teacher motivates, arranges the environment, monitors development, provides relevant and appropriate materials, and invites learners to participate in and plan literacy events and learning opportunities. Ultimately, it is the learner who builds knowledge, knowledge structures, and strategies from the enriched environment the teacher helps to create.

- As teachers monitor and support the development of reading and writing strategies, learners focus on the communication of meaning. So there is a double agenda in literacy instruction. The kids focus on what they are using reading and writing for. The teachers focus on development and use.

- Risk-taking is essential. Developing readers must be encouraged to predict and guess as they try to make sense of print. Developing writers must be encouraged to think about what they want to say, to explore genre, to invent spellings, and to experiment with punctuation. Learners need to appreciate that miscues, spelling inventions, and other imperfections are part of learning.

- Motivation is always intrinsic. Kids learn to read and write because they need and want to communicate. Extrinsic rewards have no place in a whole language classroom. Punishment for not learning is even more inappropriate.

- The most important question a teacher can ask a reader or writer is, "Does that make sense?" Learners need to be encouraged to ask the same question of themselves as they read and write.

- Materials for instruction must be whole texts that are meaningful and relevant. From the first school experiences, they must have all the characteristics of real functional language. There is no need for special texts to teach reading or writing.

- Away with exercises that chop language into bits and pieces to be practiced in isolation from a whole text!

- Predictability is the real measure of how hard a text is for a particular reader. The more predictable, the easier.

- No materials are acceptable if they divert the attention of writers from expression and readers from comprehension.

What's whole about whole language?

We can summarize what's whole in whole language in the following points:

- Whole language learning builds around whole learners learning whole language in whole situations.

- Whole language learning assumes respect for language, for the learner, and for the teacher.

- The focus is on meaning and not on language itself, in authentic speech and literacy events.

- Learners are encouraged to take risks and invited to use language, in all its varieties, for their own purposes.

- In a whole language classroom, all the varied functions of oral and written language are appropriate and encouraged.

Evaluation

In all that, whole language teachers are concerned with helping learners build underlying competence. They have no interest in getting them to behave in predetermined ways in class and on tests. For example, spelling competence is not a matter of memorizing words for the Friday spelling test, but a matter of first trying out words as they are needed in writing, and then learning the limits of invented spelling against social convention. The basic competence of children who can comprehend when they read English is not reflected in tests of word recognition or phonics "skills." Moreover, pupils can give right answers on tests for wrong reasons, and wrong answers for right reasons. Whole language teachers know that the language miscues pupils make often show their underlying competence, the strengths they are developing and testing the limits of.

Kid-watching

Before the testing movement became the multi-million dollar activity it has become, there was a developing child-study movement among researchers and educators. It's simply true that one can learn much more about pupils by carefully watching than by formal testing. Whole language teachers are constant kid-watchers. Informally, in the course of watching a child write, listening to a group of children discuss or plan together, or having a casual conversation, teachers evaluate. It even happens while children are playing. It happens more formally in one-to-one conferences with pupils about their reading or writing, as teachers make anecdotal records of what they observe. It may involve instruments like the Reading Miscue Inventory or a writing observation form. The key is that it happens in the course of ongoing classroom activities.

Whole language teachers evaluate and revise their plans on the basis of the kid-watching they do. But the most useful form of evaluation is self-evaluation. Teachers continuously evaluate themselves and their teaching. They also help pupils develop ways of evaluating their own development, of knowing when they are and when they are not successful in using language and learning through it.

Evaluation has certain general purposes in any program. It is useful in planning and modifying instruction so it will be more effective. It is also useful in getting a sense of the progress pupils have made in their growth, and some sense of the needs they have.

Most of these purposes can be accomplished through ongoing kid-watching.

At times it may be useful to use more formal devices to get indications of the strengths and weaknesses of the learners. Unfortunately, most standardized tests of reading and writing focus strongly on isolated skills and words. If they use connected texts, these are often short, disjointed, and deliberately obscure to make them harder, so that the scores are stretched out and produce a bell-shaped performance curve. To the extent that standardized tests test things other than effective use of language, they are inappropriate for judging whole language practices and initiatives, and are useless in serving the legitimate aims of evaluation.

Instead, most whole language teachers have pupils fill portfolios with their own writing, records of their reading experiences, and examples of other learning activities.

6

Developing Literacy: Whole Language The Whole Way

Whole language integrates oral and written language, and it integrates development in both with learning across the curriculum. In this chapter, notes on a more specific reading and writing curriculum will be presented. Readers should keep in mind that everything said here about developing literacy assumes that it is being done in the context of an integrated holistic curriculum.

How can whole language be implemented?

Holistic instruction shows continuous respect for language, for learners, and for teachers. It begins with everyday, useful, relevant, functional language, and moves through a full range of written language including literature in all its variety.

One major advantage whole language approaches have over others is that they don't require special instructional materials. What's required is a range of real materials in the language(s) of the learners. The key to immersion programs in second-language learning is the fact that learners are involved in real speech and literacy events. It's as simple as that, and just as important in developing literacy as it is in developing oracy (control over oral language).

Children read familiar, meaningful wholes first, predictable materials that draw on concepts and experiences they already have: signs, cereal boxes, T-shirts, and books. Soon they will spot familiar words and phrases in new wholes, and it won't be long before they are able to handle unfamiliar words and phrases in familiar uses anywhere - with no worries for the teacher about a sequence or hierarchy of skills. The curriculum is organized through shared planning between teachers and pupils around real problem-solving, real ideas, and real relevant issues. Such an authentic curriculum presents many opportunities for making sense out of print or for writing comprehensibly. You can't make sense of or through language if the language isn't all available to you. Literacy development is a matter of getting the processes together: learning, in the context of reading and writing real language, to use just enough print, language structure, and meaning, and to keep it all in the proper personal and cultural perspective. Learners need to know which available cues are most useful in a particular written context. Trial and error, risk-taking on the part of the learner, is an absolute requirement. Pupils must become more flexible as they become involved with content further removed from their direct, personal experience.

There are no whole language literacy "programs" without whole language teachers. Most crucial is the new role of the enlightened teacher who serves as guide, facilitator, and kid-watcher. Whole language teachers try to help developing readers and writers use written language to learn - to acquire, extend, and present concepts. They capitalize on the language competence and the language learning ability of children, and help make literacy an extension of natural language learning. They know their pupils well, and encourage them to collaborate with their peers. These teachers share their own expertise and knowledge with their pupils.

Preschool literacy

Literacy begins with doing what other family members do already responding to signs, logos, and labels; sharing books; scribbling notes. Many children take books to bed and cuddle them like teddy bears. There's a ready market for board books, bathable books, and books to touch, smell, and manipulate. Children who have crayons, pencils, pens, or markers experiment avidly with writing.

Objectives

- Continue to build an awareness of the functions of print - environmental print, informational reading, note writing, recreational books.

- Create literate environments with functional print everywhere and children constantly encouraged to notice it, use it, and transact with it.

- Expand children's sense of books and how to handle them. Not all children will have had access to books, magazines, and other print materials. Now is the time to give them that.

- Expand children's sense of narrative and expository texts.

- Expand their sense of the style and form of written language. Children should be read to and with. Their composition should be encouraged through dictation to teachers and paraprofessionals, and through beginning attempts at personal writing.

Parents can play a vital role at this stage. Ask them to share with their children such things as letters, forms, advertisements, magazines, signs, packages, and other literacy events. Urge them to take their children to libraries, where, as soon as they can sign their own names, they can check out their own books.

Specifics

- Provide a writing corner with lots of different things to write with and on.

- Use written language to tell children what things mean and what they are for, and encourage them to guess what written language says.

- Use written communications between school and home, and make children aware of the messages they contain. Emphasize their importance as message carriers.

- Take walks around the neighborhood and look for environmental print. Ask: "Why is the print there?" "What does it say?"

- Use children's names in the classroom to create attendance charts and to label belongings. Have children sign in and put their belongings in their personally labeled boxes or cubbies.

- Make charts and bulletin boards.

- Read to and with children individually and in small groups. Encourage them to follow, predict, read along, and even take over if they choose.

- Get lots of books: response books, activity books, wordless books.

- Create centers for listening to records or tapes and for writing grocery lists, notes, and picture captions.

- Encourage kids to play at reading and writing.

- Highlight the value of literacy during role-playing as children read recipes and cook, go to the comer store with a shopping list, or dress up at the clothes center where they write sales tickets or follow patterns.

Beginning literacy

The term "beginning literacy" here refers only to the beginning of a concerted school effort to support growth into literacy. It fosters children's pride and confidence in their language(s) and their growing literacy. Teaching and learning builds from whole to part, encouraging school beginners to be self-confident risk-takers.

Objectives

- Support developing awareness of print and its functions.

- Support the transition into productive reading.

- Build strategies, not specifics: meaning-seeking, predicting, inferencing, sampling, confirming, self-correcting in reading; inventing spellings and experimenting with forms to serve their functions in writing.

- Cultivate the alphabetic principle, not specific phonics.

- Develop risk-taking. In whole language the teacher is monitor, cheerleader, co-reader, and facilitator of beginning literacy reading and writing activities.

Specifics

- Make the classroom itself a literate environment in which functional, meaningful, relevant language is everywhere.

- With pupils, label centers and write charts for rules, attendance, and jobs.

- Create a gallery of biographies of the children, written and read by them.

- Make charts and bulletin boards open-ended. When appropriate, have children add to them with letters from grandparents, favorite logos, book jackets they've made, precious collections, etc.

- Create stores with boxes, cartons, and signs, as well as a classroom post office where each child has a box for receiving mail and messages.

- Get the kids involved in reading whole meaningful texts right from the beginning. Wordless picture books such as *The Red Balloon* or *Pancakes for Breakfast* help to build a sense of books and of narrative.

- Encourage children to dictate stories or experiences, individually or in groups, to an adult who writes for them. Then have the children read back their own texts. These may be rewritten on charts for further use, or bound at a classroom publishing center.

- Choose one or more read-along activities:

    o A common home read-along has the child sitting on an adult's lap looking at the book the adult is reading aloud. The adult stops or fades out periodically and lets the child take over. There are now commercial versions of this lap method that promote shared book experiences in school.

    o Many whole language teachers set up listening centers where children can listen through earphones to tapes or records while following the text in a book.

    o Others use "big book" versions of popular books that allow several children to see the same text and join in a choral reading with a leader - the teacher, another adult, or a classmate. Several companies now offer big book kits that include normal-sized copies along with the big book.

    o Assisted reading is a more formal read-along approach in which the teacher first reads with the child and then gradually shifts to merely supporting and assisting as the child reads the familiar story/text.

o Sing-along charts and choral reading of poems also enrich co-reading in the classroom.

Reading and writing

The best books at this stage are predictable books. Their familiar content and structure, and the often repetitious, cyclical sequencing make them predictable. *This is the House That Jack Built* or *I Know an Old Lady Who Swallowed a Fly* are good examples. It's easy for kids to get a sense of where the book is going and to predict what is coming next. Fortunately, young children seem to love rereading familiar predictable materials, which gives them lots of productive, self-motivated practice.

From the beginning, children write for themselves as well as dictate to teachers. They write predictable books of their own in frank imitation of the patterns of some of their favorites. They tape their own singalongs and choral readings to add to their taped-book collections. Reading and writing develop together and support each other. Young writers learn to read like writers: they notice surprising spellings, become alert to style and structure, and know that books have authors because they've experienced authoring themselves.

They also integrate reading and writing experiences into their thematic units and their search for knowledge across the curriculum. So they learn to read and write expository language as well. They learn to enjoy and create a good story, but they also learn to describe, to report, to raise questions and answer them, to share real experiences. They write letters, keep journals, make signs, labels, and lists. They keep records of their own physical growth, and the growth and food intake of classroom pets. They read the school lunch menu, the TV guide, the weather report, and keep the class up to date on the latest information.

Beginners are encouraged to take risks. When they write they spell words as best they can, inventing if necessary, but using the words they need when they need them rather than sticking with those they are sure they can spell. Their reading miscues are celebrated if they contribute to making sense and show developing strategies. No one is perfect, and sense rather than error-free performance is the main point of reading. The teacher helps them see that they should not tolerate nonsense when they read.

The teacher also monitors development through close observation. The children are growing into readers and writers. From the beginning, the reading and writing is theirs through authentic literacy events for real purposes. They have and maintain a sense of ownership - they are not tenants in someone else's literacy program. They aren't acquiring skills for later use. Rather, they are reading and writing because they need and want to do so.

Handwriting

The act of producing writing is laborious for young children and requires a great deal of physical coordination. That's the reason for using manuscript writing. Cursive writing takes more coordination and is more prone to illegibility, particularly for beginners. Even for adults, cursive handwriting becomes so idiosyncratic, so personalized, that it may become illegible. Typewriters and word processors have largely replaced handwritten letters and written texts in business.

In the beginning, composition can simply involve young pupils dictating to an adult who transcribes for later reading. Also, word processors with easy-to-learn software have been successfully used with school beginners in recent years: they take much of the drudgery out of the writing and children produce much longer texts. A few English schools are now using a simple five button keyboard, the Quinkey.

Whole language teachers understand that handwriting is not a skill that can be learned first and then used. Instruction in letter formation is built into real literacy events. Control will take a while, and development will be characterized by miscues and imperfections. Although there are many variations in physical coordination, teachers encourage all kids to write and keep on writing even if it's hard to do so legibly. Nothing discourages struggling young writers so much as a bulletin board full of near perfect but copied exercises with a label something like "Our Best Work."

Left-handed pupils need special support and encouragement. Left-handed writing doesn't need to look right-handed. It has characteristics of its own, since the writing hand will be in a different position relative to the body and the paper. Furthermore, left-handed writers are at a disadvantage learning from and watching right-handed teachers, particularly if the teachers are insensitive.

Fortunately, experienced kid-watchers easily spot how writing does or doesn't contribute to effective expression. They keep coordination, handedness, legibility, and conformity to conventions in perspective.

Developmental literacy

Developmental literacy encompasses the major part of school programs: the expansion of efficiency and effectiveness in readers and writers, and of flexibility in using literacy for various purposes. Again, developing readers and writers must be involved in authentic literacy events and in a wide range of real comprehensible texts, and they must be in control of their own use and development of literacy.

Objectives

- Build pupils' level of confidence and encourage risk-taking. Pupils self-select materials to read, strive to comprehend what they read, and risk using writing to communicate.

- Expand pupils' flexibility and help them broaden and refine their taste and breadth of interests.

- Support the development of effective expression and comprehension strategies.

- Help pupils build efficient reading and writing in a wide range of functional contexts.

- Support pupils' growth in their ability to learn through written language.

- Build a love of reading and writing so that pupils will choose to do both during their leisure time, as sources of pleasure and aesthetic satisfaction.

Specifics

These are the keys: lots of reading and writing, risk-taking to try new functions for reading and writing, focusing on meaning. If these three essentials aren't present, no matter how many specific whole language activities are used, it will not be a successful whole language curriculum.

Self-selection

Pupils are helped to broaden the scope and range of their

reading and writing and to build the special strategies needed for different kinds of texts used for different purposes. It helps if students know what they want to know, what questions they want answered, and what problems they need to solve.

Sustained time for reading and writing

Many diligent teachers find it hard to stay out of the kids' way. We think we're not teaching if we're not telling them something, or at least asking them something. But watching them as they read and write is often more helpful. Of course teachers need to know what the kids are doing and be there when they need (and particularly when they ask for) help. But much can be accomplished through regular individual conferences where the pupils share their reading and writing with the teacher, through small group interactions, and through peer editing conferences.

Journals

Teachers respond regularly to what kids write. As they get older, pupils may prefer to turn their journals into private diaries, and they should decide whether or not the teacher will read and respond.

A variation from Japan uses writing to have children get in touch with themselves. There teachers believe that beginning writing should narrate the child's own experiences, to help put the child in touch with his or her feelings. They do not respond except to comment on the extent to which the young writers are coming to grips with the experiences they've had and their reactions to them.

Process writing

Donald Graves, Donald Murray, and others have developed this approach. Young writers are allowed time for pre-writing, for thinking about and planning what they will say. Then there is time for the writing. Finally, there is time to share with classmates what was written. Getting responses from a real peer audience is helpful in revision.

Revision

Many things kids write - notes to friends, quick responses to experiences, jottings, or journal entries - serve their purposes in their initial forms. Revisions are reserved for stories, reports, personal narratives, or expressions of personal response to ideas or experiences, whatever is intended for sharing with a wider audience. Revision helps make the text more comprehensible and acceptable to the intended audience. It also helps writers say what they intend to say. The process of revision also leads to more effective strategies for expression and to more successful texts. It's important to develop a sense of what kinds of text need revision under what circumstances, and what the best devices are for revising each text type.

Spelling, punctuation, and forms

There is simply no doubt that, as long as they keep on writing meaningfully, young writers will move toward conventional spelling and punctuation, and control over the forms of stories, letters, and other writing genres.

Spelling: Beginners will generate spellings so minimal and unique that even they may not always be able to read what they've written. But soon they will develop predictable consistencies so that both they and the teacher can read what they write. In English, for example, vowels will initially be left out, and then some vowels will consistently represent vowel sounds that are not necessarily the conventional ones. Soon even readers who are not as experienced as teachers with invented spellings will be able to figure out what the writer is saying. Next, developing writers will realize that the spelling in the material they read is standardized. This may inhibit their writing, as they avoid using words they're not sure of. But if they feel supported and encouraged, they will continue to invent spellings for new words they need, while using their reading and writing experience to move toward conventional spelling. Studies of misspellings among young writers show that they are almost entirely confined to words being used for the first time. Frequently used words are only infrequently misspelled.

Punctuation: The same story. If they read and if they write, kids develop a sense for where to punctuate. There's no way to rush it, but there's no need to hurry anyway. Just don't tell kids that periods come at the end of sentences and then teach them that sentences end with periods!

Forms of writing: Pupils learn about basic forms of writing by using them. For example, they learn to write a letter, for either formal or informal purposes, by writing real letters to real people for real reasons. Whole language classrooms have mailboxes, and children write to each other. They are also encouraged to write to relatives, to friends, or to companies for information. Arranging for written exchanges with other classrooms or groups provides real literacy events involving handwriting.

Meaning in reading

In reading, meaning is always both input and output. First, wanting to comprehend is half the battle. Of course the conceptual load must be appropriate and the writing must be quality stuff, but pupils will work hard and extend themselves to understand texts that are important to them. Pupils are active in their own learning and transactive with the texts they read.

It's important to recognize the limits of textbooks. Good ones support the curriculum, but holistic teachers do not abuse and misuse textbooks by equating them with the curriculum. They use them as limited resources and build cooperative relationships with librarians, publishers, and authors, so that students can become aware of the large variety of written language resources they can use to build the knowledge they are looking for.

Skills and strategies

The technology of reading boasts of objective skills and drills. Instead, whole language classrooms offer development of comprehension strategies. These focus on the ways living, breathing people organize graphic, syntactic, and meaning cues for making sense of real whole language. The human mind constantly develops strategies for organizing the information it needs for all kinds of purposes. Whole language teachers use strategy lessons to expand on strengths and help build strategies.

Strategy lessons require the use of meaningful language passages in the context of real literacy events. Many different types are rapidly being developed. Here is an example:

A teacher notes that some pupils tend to substitute *what* for *that* when they read. There are also occasional *when/then* and *where/there* substitutions, often in situations where either word would fit. Other than drilling on isolated words, the teacher finds - or writes - a meaningful passage in which each time only one of the words can fit and make sense. The pupils read the passage to strengthen their self-correction strategies. With each miscue, they discover something is wrong and are led by the text to correct. But this strategy lesson also helps them become better predictors. It's important not to call their attention to the words in isolation, since that would compound the problem by strengthening an association between the words.

Metacognition

Recently, some researchers have discussed metacognition: knowing what you know and how you know it. They argue that comprehension and expression will be aided by getting kids to talk about the literacy processes. The idea that kids are helped by being taught *first* about language is not consistent with the basic whole language principle. However, it probably is true that as kids become literate they get some key insights about reading and writing which subsequently make their learning easier.

Among these are:

- Language is always supposed to make sense. So in reading you know you've been successful if you understand what you read. In writing you keep rereading what you've written to make sure it makes sense.

- No one can understand everything. This reality can help kids maintain their self-confidence and develop some sense of when their lack of comprehension is the fault of the text, their lack of background, or other sources besides their own reading ability.

- Personal meanings may differ from the meanings of the community, in minor or major ways. Pupils need to internalize these shared meanings while maintaining and perfecting their personal meanings.

Teachable moments

They're the best for metacognition. Sometimes one or more

pupils want to talk about language. Sometimes teachers can evoke curiosity about an aspect of language. In either case, the goal of the teacher is to help pupils use their insights to build comprehension and expression strategies.

Strategies across the curriculum

Learners need to develop special strategies for comprehending the kinds of text found in math, science, social studies, and the arts. For instance, it helps when they discover that math story problems need to be read in several ways for several purposes:

- Deciding what information is being sought.

- Laying out a solution strategy and deciding on appropriate equations and computations.

- Getting specific information and checking the potential solution against the problem.

Literacy development in a content area

Here is a general approach:

- Review the general and special uses of reading and writing in the content area.

- Consider what kinds of written language texts are common in the field, particularly those pupils may not have encountered before: for example, maps, charts, recipes, directions, job sheets, scripts.

- Think through and list what strategies, background knowledge, and special resources are needed to reproduce and comprehend the texts the field uses.

- Determine where kids are in being able to meet these needs.

- Plan the double agenda that will build the necessary language strategies while building knowledge in the subject area.

7

Revaluing: An Alternative To Remediation

When pupils don't do well in a technologized reading and writing program, it's assumed there must be something wrong with *them*. The language of medical pathology will describe it: reading disabilities, dyslexia, diagnosis, clinics, prescriptions, treatments, remediation. We blame their eyes, their brains, their central nervous systems, their diets, their noisy homes or their quiet ones, their neglectful parents or their over-anxious ones. But after all the diagnosis, the treatment is remarkably uniform: take two phonics exercises three times a day. That's because the pathology of reading failure knows nothing about the reading process or reading development.

Writing deficiencies don't often cause alarm before high school. The early assumption is that if kids can't read there's no point in expecting them to write. In high schools we "know" that students write poorly because they haven't been taught to write correctly. Resulting exercises in writing form, spelling, and handwriting produce even more uptight writers who try to write by the rules instead of trying to say something in writing. College remedial writing courses continue to be atomistic and negative and to focus on form rather than meaningful language.

Putting it bluntly, a whole language perspective is opposed to all this atomistic negative language learning. If young humans haven't succeeded in becoming literate in school, something must be wrong with the program: *it needs remediation, not they.*

In the meantime, there are lots of ineffective and troubled readers and writers. You easily recognize them. They are often in conflict with themselves and are usually their own worst enemies. By now they try to read and write by busily attacking words and looking up spellings. They mistrust their own language strategies and become dependent on teachers to tell them what to do as they read and write. They are reluctant to take the necessary risks, with the result that their reading and writing looks far less competent than it actually is. They believe that everyone knows they are literacy failures, and they act the part.

They believe there are two kinds of people in school: those who can read and write and those who can't and never will. They think the skills and drill exercises that never work for them always work for the good readers, who never have any problems. It's all their own fault - a sign of something defective, inferior, or bad. They suffer from the "next word" syndrome. Every word they're not sure of is proof that they are bad readers. Good readers always know the next word. All words are equal, aren't they? So they sound out every proper name, as well as the important concept-carrying words. They don't expect things to make sense. Reading is the tedious task of trying to get all the words right. They believe that good writers are perfect spellers too, so what's the use of even trying.

They also suffer from the "I can't remember" syndrome. Good readers have total recall of everything they read, of course. Since these readers never do, they're defective. Troubled writers have never heard of "composition at the point of utterance." They believe good writers have the whole of what they will write in their heads before they begin.

It's easy to see how the technology of reading instruction, the tests, texts, and exercises, build these self-destructive and inaccurate views of literacy.

Children who have trouble in reading and writing do have strengths - making sense of language is natural for people. But through lack of self-confidence and overkill on isolated skills, they don't recognize their own strengths. They think their use of legitimate comprehension and expression strategies is cheating. They feel guilty if they make sense of what they're reading without sounding out the words, if they skip words and enjoy their reading without worrying about remembering everything.

Objectives

There are only two objectives of a revaluing program:

- To support pupils in revaluing themselves as language learners, and to get them to believe they are capable of becoming fully literate.

- To support pupils in revaluing reading and writing as functional, meaningful whole language processes rather than as sequences of sub-skills to be memorized.

Revaluing is essential. If those pupils are to become literate, they must lose the loser mentality. They must find the strength and confidence to take the necessary risks, to make the literacy choices, and to enter into functional literacy events. Whole language teaching helps pupils value what they can do and not be defeated by what they can't do; it helps them trust themselves and their linguistic intuitions, to become self-reliant in their sense of what they are reading.

Whole, relevant, meaningful language can help them move away from next-word fear, phonics, and word attacks. It can help them build productive meaning-seeking strategies. Eventually they will come to realize that making sense is all that reading and writing are about.

Specifics

Patience is a key word. Severely labeled pupils will take a while to turn around and start believing in themselves. The transition will require a building up of their understanding of what print can do for them in the context of real literacy events. In such contexts, they will gradually reveal to themselves and their teachers the strengths that have been hidden by the heavy layer of their own defeatism, brought on by inappropriate overuse of word-attack skills. But it will take time. Their scars are deep; the effect of years of pathological treatment and remediation will not wear off easily.

Beginner whole language activities are appropriate at any age, provided the content and interest level are relevant to the learners. Teenagers interested in cars can dictate to a teacher or tutor how to change a tire. When it has been typed or written, teacher and pupil can read it together. Perhaps this could initiate an auto mechanic's log or journal written by a group of pupils for their own use or that of others. Having troubled readers read along with a recorded reader, or read highly predictable materials are also useful techniques.

Materials of great interest are likely to be most predictable for learners, and the range of interests and experiences will become increasingly broad with age. Predictability will differ from person to person, since it depends on interests, culture, hobbies, vocations, values, and life experiences. Resourceful teachers get newspapers, magazines, books, forms, menus, or any other written texts to which they can point specific learners for specific purposes. Bless caring librarians! Bless patient teachers who never flag in believing that readers can predict and comprehend when they read about things they know! Their charges are prone to giving up easily and need constant reassurance.

Even with highly meaningful materials, it takes time for kids to revalue themselves and the processes of literacy. Teachers must expect some setbacks and even some trauma as learners struggle with themselves to accept that getting the gist of what they are reading is more important than getting each word right. Helping kids revalue themselves is largely helping them put themselves together. Over the years they've been fractionated, and have lost the sense of the whole. Keeping them involved, always, in a search for meaning eventually brings them together.

Pupils can also be encouraged to learn from their own miscues. They can work in pairs, taking turns reading and tape-recording their reading. At first the teacher listens to the tape, asks them about the miscues they notice they made, and encourages them to evaluate what they did right. Later they can work with their partners without the teacher's help. Self-appraisal helps to legitimize the miscue-making, guessing, predicting, and inferencing they are doing. The importance of self-correction in seeking to make sense of the text becomes clear. High-quality miscues are highlighted and suggestions are made that strategies which worked in some places could have been used in others to overcome similar difficulties. Working in pairs helps kids realize that others share their problems. Most of all, this self-analysis gets them to confront the reality of their own reading, including its strengths as well as its weaknesses, and that will make them question the stereotype of themselves as total losers in literacy.

These pupils often show progress in revaluing themselves as writers before they do as readers. They start keeping journals, and the entries get longer and longer. They are surprised and pleased to discover that people enjoy hearing about episodes in their lives, and they begin to write long accounts of interesting experiences. Writing is easy for new believers in themselves because it demands no skill prerequisites. Spelling, handwriting, and mechanics are learned on the job in the process of expressing: And their writing goes through the same remarkable rapid development that younger writers show, provided the teacher is there to be an interested consumer. The teacher must support and cheer them on and not wipe out their first efforts and early enthusiasm with red-penciled sarcasm. It's not lowering any standards to compliment a fourteen-year-old beginning writer on his first coherent six page story, even if it does have some misspelled words and non-standard punctuation. If the writing continues, the rest will follow. If it doesn't, there won't be anything to spell or punctuate.

Preventive whole language

If kids are in whole language classrooms with whole language teachers right from the beginning, there are going to be a lot fewer readers and writers in trouble. Whole language teachers work at developing the full range of language functions in the context of the culture(s) of the learners. They are effective kid-watchers who see quickly when kids are not developing and find alternatives that will turn them on and get them moving. Most important, they believe in kids, and they believe kids have what it takes to become literate. They won't blame them for their lack of success. Rather, they'll build on their strengths and encourage them to believe in themselves and their ability to become literate.

8

Reality: The State Of The Language Arts

We're a long way from where we should be. Whole language teachers, schools, and policies in the English-speaking nations are increasing in numbers, but the three are not always found together. Sometimes school policy-makers have committed themselves, but the teachers were never involved and are now unable or unwilling to implement whole language. More common, whole language teachers alone and in small numbers try building a whole language curriculum amidst unsupportive or even hostile administrator and curricular policies. Many parents support whole language administrative policies and teacher initiatives, but there is not yet a popular movement. Ultimately, if whole language is going to become the dominant school approach to teaching and learning, most parents must come to see the advantage of its humanistic/ scientific base and its positive view of children and learning, and the potential it has for expanding both the effectiveness of their children's use of oral and written language and their ability to learn through language.

Well-developed ideas like whole language ought to be causing excitement, discussion, and controversy. They should be reflected in policies curriculum guides, published classroom materials, teacher education programs, and the professional and popular press. They are in many parts of the English-speaking world. For instance, language across the curriculum is a central concept in secondary programs in New Zealand, Britain, Canada, Australia, and such countries as Singapore, where English is one of the official languages. The United States, however, is lagging far behind.

What is happening in whole language?

New Zealand

For its single national school authority, whole language *is* the policy in New Zealand. Its secondary language program aims to:

- Increase students' ability to understand and use language effectively.

- Extend their imaginative and emotional responsiveness to and through language.

- Extend their awareness of ideas and values through language.

Teachers are expected to develop curricula practices that are consistent with these broad aims. They are asked to plan with their students "an appropriate range of language situations arising from and widening the students' own experience" - that is, expanding the range of language situations in which they are confident and competent. Teachers are expected to plan language activities based on students' everyday lives, widening interests, and developmental needs.

Evaluation is based on a full range of language use in different situations, rather than on tests: logs, folders, and tapes of work; records of teacher/student conferences; careful and continued observation of such activities as role-playing, group discussion, the making of collages and sound pictures; informal tests; assessment by audiences of class plays, debates, and other such language activities.

Great Britain

In 1975, the Bullock Committee, an official representation of the British government, issued its report called *A Language for Life*. It called for major changes in objectives, curricula, and methodology in education based on insights into the relationships among language, thinking, and learning. The report elevated concern for development of language and thinking to the level of policy. It was widely discussed in many English-speaking countries.

Since then, schools and local education authorities have established school language policies in Great Britain, Canada, Australia, and New Zealand. The school's acceptance of all forms of language and its commitment to support home languages as well as English have been clarified. The joint responsibility of the entire school staff for language development has been articulated. These policies make language a major focus of concern and put it at the center of the curriculum.

Also, many British teacher education programs have made language a major focus. James Britton, Nancy Martin, John Dixon, Harold Rosen, and Margaret Spencer are prominent British teacher educators who have played a major role in ensuring that British primary and secondary teachers have the background in language and learning they need to integrate language development with learning through language. There is now a broad process of holistic innovation there, though the *term* whole language is only beginning to be heard.

Canada

There has been a strong movement in Canada for whole language at many different levels. *English Language Arts I-VI* is the official policy statement of the Direction Générale de Development Pédagogique, Ministère de l'Education for the Province of Quebec. It mandates a "whole language, child-centered, integrated approach." Its core is a parallel series of theoretical assumptions and instructional principles. For example:

Theoretical assumption: language learning is an active developmental process which occurs over a period of time.

Instructional principle: children need time to internalize the process by actively engaging in the process of speaking, listening, reading, and writing.

Theoretical assumption: language arts must occur and flourish in literate environments where language users are free to discover and to realize their intentions.

Instructional principle: children need to be encouraged to take risks and need to experience varied opportunities for language use.

The teacher is asked to create meaningful contexts for learning, "invitational, emulative environments" which:

- Provide integrated experiences with the language arts.

- Influence the children's attitude toward language, while

promoting development through developmentally appropriate varied opportunities for language use.

- Support the natural process of learning, building language and extending knowledge, shaping meaning, and sharing the world of language.

The whole language, child-centered, integrated approach ties broad objectives to related content. For the student to view English as a dynamic and living language, a wide range of stories, poems, plays, books, magazines, and newspapers should be at hand. Monitoring achievement includes two forms: response indicators like "reads every day," "recreates stories"; value indicators like "enjoys the different uses of language by authors." Evaluation suggestions include use of observation, formal and informal tests, parent and student conferences, school records, checklists, questionnaires, inventories, and tapes of oral language. Self-evaluation is integrally involved in the process and is encouraged.

A team of teachers in Edmonton, Alberta, has developed a working paper that has these premises:

Language Arts must be integrated based on interdependence of listening, speaking, reading, and writing and the need for people to have language to communicate with others and understand and control their daily experiences. Language and thought develop together and subject area concepts develop at the same time as pupils' ability to express their understandings through reading and writing. Language is an active process learned through its use.

The statement of "Language Arts Outcomes" is both broad enough and specific enough to give direction to teachers and planners. It does not confuse trivial activities with reasons for learning. Here are some examples of their objectives:

- Students can and will read, listen, and view for recreation and information.

- Students are able to use language to discuss when constructing their own messages and analyzing the messages of others.

However, the Edmonton group recognizes that a whole language, child-centered, integrated approach will not succeed unless teachers understand it, accept it enthusiastically, and are free to implement it.

Whole language views are represented in official documents and innovative practices all across Canada - in British Columbia, Alberta, Manitoba, Saskatchewan, Ontario, Quebec, Nova Scotia, New Brunswick, and Newfoundland. The David Livingston School in inner city Winnipeg has become a center of whole language teaching. Its staff and a group of associated Winnipeg educators have played a major role in creating a grassroots movement in Canada through in-service work.

The United States

There is a strong whole language movement in the United States, but it is harder to see against the background of irrational demands for excellence that only translate into standardized test scores, back-to-basics movements, and pressures for narrowed curricula from moral majority and elitist groups. John Goodlad calls a "monstrous hypocrisy" the "gap between rhetoric of individual flexibility, originality, and creativity in our educational goals and the cultivation of these goals in our schools ..." He says that "the emphasis on individual performance and achievement would be more conducive to cheating than to development of moral integrity," and concludes that "back to basics is where we've always been." In reading, he sees overwhelming focus on textbooks and workbooks, with little actual reading and writing. Excluding "the common practice of students taking turns reading from a common text," reading accounts for only 6% of elementary class time and trails off to 3% in junior high school and 2% in senior high.

Unlike the other countries we've looked at, whole language remains overwhelmingly a teachers' movement in the United States. Only a limited number of curriculum workers, administrators, and teacher educators actively support it.

How can policy become practice?

What must be done? The key problem is turning whole language policy into practical reality in the classroom. After all, whole language ideas and concepts become reality only at the point where a teacher is alone with a group of learners. Only there does a whole language, child-centered, integrated approach really exist.

But doing so won't be easy. Mechanistic, technological packages are popular among many school administrators. One American federally funded educational laboratory boasted that it took only a day to train (their word) teachers to use their program. Training consisted mostly of rehearsing the use of the script, which had an invariant format. Teachers were admonished not to deviate from the program in any way, for any child, for any reason. Another mastery learning program literally requires teachers to sign a loyalty oath to the program.

Whole language can't be packaged in a kit or bound between the covers of textbooks or workbooks. It certainly can't be scripted. There's no use building a whole language "program" per se, it is a child-centered, integrated approach that cannot be implemented without the support of the teachers. Teachers must reach their own informed professional decisions. They - with the kids - create whole language classrooms. Responsible administrators and curriculum planners have learned that teachers deserve the same humane, patient understanding as the pupils they teach. They can't be, and shouldn't be, coerced or intimidated.

"Support for Instructional Development" is the name of a new type of in-service program in the Albuquerque public schools. A major element is the support of study groups. Teachers are paid an hourly rate to participate in a series of seven or eight sessions. They are asked to read articles, keep journals to reflect on their reading, and ask questions. One series of lectures, discussions, and demonstrations focused on: beliefs about reading; word perception and using predictable materials; the schema theory and the sociopsycholinguistic nature of reading; making reading easy/literature as the content of reading; the reading/writing connection; miscue analysis; synthesis and reactions.

The support also extends to classroom demonstrations, in-service to entire school faculties, lunch symposia, individual staff/teacher conferences, location of materials and/or information, arranging visitations by teachers to other classrooms and other schools. This way more and more whole language teachers become willing and able to share what they know. Seeing what peers have done makes clear to novices that whole language works with kids exactly like the ones in their classes. Also, peer support lowers the risks for the teacher being supported because the peer has no intimidating authority.

American school systems might borrow ideas from England, where Moira McKenzie of the Inner London Education Authority runs courses. Some classroom teachers are released from classes to attend; some attend after a full day's teaching. The ILEA designates a few as "post-holders in language." These are regular classroom teachers who have the responsibility of sharing ideas with their colleagues and supporting them in turn. The course creates a continuous, relatively non-threatening source of ideas, support and impetus for change.

In Great Britain, Australia, New Zealand, and Canada it is common to "second" teachers to a teacher center, a special project, or a teacher education program. The teacher performs a different professional role and at the same time acquires new insights and competences. Such borrowings happen in the United States too, but less frequently and less officially.

Curriculum guidelines

The Quebec curriculum guide and course of study provides an excellent model for a system-wide whole language, child-centered, integrated approach. Composing such a document takes as wide a range of participation as possible. Classroom teachers, specialists and support staff, curriculum workers and administrators, parents and other interested members of the community are all prime candidates for membership in committees and study groups. The support of teacher educators should also be enlisted. The process of developing a guideline is likely to be as important as the end product, and those who have had a hand in its development may make all the difference in its implementation later.

In presenting the completed guide to those who weren't involved, the developers should explain what decisions were made, why the guide is what it is, and what changes to the system the planners visualize. Teachers should explain to teachers, principals to principals, parents to parents.

Here are some of the things you might expect in a curriculum guide:

- A *language policy* that deals with the broad objectives of expanding oral and written language effectiveness in both English and mother tongues. It should deal with general principles such as integrating language development with learning through language. But it should also tackle specific concerns of the population served, such as treatment of minority dialects. Bryant Fillion suggests that a language policy should deal with such things as: how students are required, encouraged, and permitted to use language; what happens as a result of their language use; and what they are taught - directly and indirectly - about language. Fillion argues for each school to explicate its language policy to demonstrate that it promotes "real language development and the effective use of language as a tool for learning."

- A *base of humanistic/scientific principles* to be used for choosing materials, planning instruction, organizing classrooms, and evaluating pupil progress and the approach itself.

- *Methods* schools will use to expand and support learning. It should indicate the role of the teacher in supporting, facilitating, and monitoring language development, and suggest ways of integrating the language arts and establishing the double agenda of learning through language while learning language. Specific suggestions for organizing thematic units and for appropriate unit topics and resources will always be helpful. It should provide lists of fiction and non-fiction tides that can support unit topics. It should suggest appropriate language experiences (speech and literacy events) for units.

- *Recommendations* for time and space for a whole language, child-centered, integrated approach. Teachers are always worried that pupils will not have enough to do without workbooks and skills exercises. A guide should suggest a variety of ways to organize time in relationship to ongoing thematic units, so that pupils are productively involved and the teacher can monitor how they are using their time. It should also suggest how to develop centers, arrange desks, and make materials available and accessible so they will facilitate activity in an orderly manner.

- A *means of evaluation* is always a major concern, particularly in the United States with its almost obsessive preoccupation with the use of standardized tests, and any guide must address the problem. There are models, developed by a group of teachers, which suggests a variety of informal and formal procedures and devices for monitoring the progress pupils are making in language and conceptual development.

The curriculum guide should be considered provisional and there should be a continuous process of revision and evaluation. This will permit the whole staff to feel that the curriculum is theirs and that their experience in facilitating whole language is important in shaping this integrated approach.

Whole language schools

Increasingly, whole schools are shifting to whole language, as a faculty decides that a whole language approach is the way to go. Sometimes support is available from the local education authority or from a university faculty. In a few cases, parents and teachers have argued that if a basics program is a parental choice for some children, a positive holistic program should be a parental choice for others.

Liz Waterland describes how an apprenticeship approach was established in Northborough School in Cambridgeshire, England:

No one in the school had used anything other than a conventional, largely skill-based program ... There were the parents to worry about; their expectation would be that their children would follow the traditional pattern ... There were the resources to consider. It was obvious that reading schemes were, with few exceptions, no longer appropriate. Had we sufficient books to use? What about children's writing?

We already had a language curriculum. Now I wanted to abandon that plan; plainly the staff would also need to understand and support, at least in theory ... It was the fact that my head teacher gave me his wholehearted support ... that finally convinced me it could be done.

It was in this spirit that I began to attempt to turn theory into practice, first ... by myself feeling my way into it. Within a term, so successful was the children's response that colleagues in the rest of the school began using the apprenticeship approach with their classes. Two years later we were offering help to and sharing ideas with other schools throughout Cambridgeshire.

Waterland informed the parents right from the beginning, and asked them to support the initiative by reading with their children. Guidance was provided in a booklet: " ... the home can offer time, individual attention, consistent support, and loving concern; the school can offer expertise, suitable texts, and understanding of progression."

The staff of David Livingstone School in Winnipeg, Manitoba, led by principal Orin Cochrane, plan and continuously revise the program. When they began, they had the support of Ethel Buchanan, who operates a teacher center. Team-teaching is common. The school is in an inner- city area with low income families, many of them native Canadians. With like-minded teachers, the staff forms a support group that provides courses and in-service workshops for teachers and administrators in other schools and other parts of the country.

The federally funded Chapter 1 Reading Program became the focus for initiating a whole language, child centered, integrated approach in Albuquerque, New Mexico. Professor Bess Altwerger was selected to work a third of her time helping the staff of the Alamosa School. Administrator Virginia Resta facilitated and supported the plans. The school had recognized a great need for improvement in its literacy curriculum. With support from the principal, a group of teachers volunteered to provide a whole language initiative. An on-site "facilitating teacher" was selected for coordination. Non-Chapter 1 teachers were encouraged to observe and participate, but there was no pressure.

In each example above, several key things were present:

- A staff that wanted to change to a positive, humanistic/scientific approach.

- A core of leadership within the group or supportive of it.

- The support of administrators who were not afraid to share power with teachers.

- Informed parents who supported the child centered integrated approach.

- A knowledge-base that was continually expanded by the staff, who were actively committed to developing a whole language curriculum.

- Teachers who viewed themselves as professionals, who

were not afraid to take risks, and who were willing to take responsibility for their classrooms.

- Pupils who participated in planning their education, who were actively engaged in their own development and the pursuit of knowledge, and who liked going to school.

Helping teachers change

Being a whole language teacher raises the level of professional authority and responsibility. It means accepting the responsibility of staying informed, of developing a sound base for classroom planning, practice, and decision-making. It is important, therefore, that support be continuous and long-term. Teachers must not feel abandoned after they've been convinced to change what they're doing, but before they know what to do instead.

It would be unfair, unrealistic, and unwise to expect teachers to make abrupt changes. They have reasons for what they do now. They know how successful (and unsuccessful) they are. They can predict from past experience how well something they do will work (and not work). Trying out new ways of doing things is risky business. The results are unpredictable. Teachers need support in setting their own pace and planning their own transition. If they need to cling to textbooks for a while, if they're not quite ready to let go of their formal spelling programs, that's all right. Conferences and support groups, support staff observations, and visits to other classrooms will help them think through what they are hanging onto, where they are inconsistent and where not, and how to keep moving ahead to more effective teaching.

9

Whole Language: Not Without A Whole Language Teacher

In the end there is no getting away from this truth: it's one class at a time, just you and your kids.

Most whole language teachers are not in whole language schools. They are often alone and frequently considered by their colleagues and administrators as hard-working and effective, but misguided.

The lucky ones have a colleague or two who share their convictions. More often, they have to seek out teachers in other schools and districts to share their successes and failures, their victories and defeats. They find their associates through support groups, and through whole language newsletters and other publications.

What makes a whole language teacher?

Commitment

Becoming a whole language teacher is a bold decision for many. Once the decision has been made that being a professional means accepting responsibility for using the best available knowledge to educate every learner to the fullest extent possible, then prescriptive teaching material is out. The welfare of children cannot be left to authors of basals and standardized tests. The methods or materials that are inconsistent with the teacher's best professional judgment must go.

For some, this bold decision comes even before the first teaching job, as a knowledge of whole language and a belief base is formed at the university. These teachers only have to learn how to do it, in the reality of a real classroom. For others the decision comes later, brought about by reading, by an in-service workshop, or by interaction with colleagues. They come to realize that they've been satisfied to accept limited success as the fault of pupils rather than of wrong methods, materials, exercises, and basals.

Some teachers come to realize that they've been whole language teachers for years - a liberating discovery! They are justified in their professional judgments. It's relatively easy for them to give up the things they've been doing, things they never really believed in, and to expand on what they always, in their hearts, knew was right. As they connect theory with practice, they put heart and head together and are greatly strengthened in their teaching.

Transition

For many teachers, the transition is pretty scary. They become whole language teachers quietly, step by step, ruffling as few feathers as possible and easing themselves and their pupils into it. The teacher's own style, the degree of flexibility in the school district requirements and mandates, the nature of the community and the school population, traditions in the school and community, and the courage (or brashness) of the teacher all play a role, making each transition unique.

Here is one possible sequence for a teacher to follow:

First, assess your program.

- Is your present program not helping your pupils to become literate?

- Would a move toward whole language be better for your kids?

- Are you reasonably satisfied with your reading and writing program but concerned about integrating language development with the rest of the curriculum?

Next, consider what you are already doing that is consistent with a whole language, child-centered, integrated approach.

- Do you use thematic units? Is your classroom a literate environment? Is it organized around flexible activity centers?

- Are your pupils involved in authentic speech and literacy events? Do they help plan their school experiences and engage in problem-solving?

- Do you use a wide range of materials and involve pupils in a range of language functions? Are the materials easily accessible to them? Is there a lot of functional reading and writing going on?

- Are parents informed of what you are doing? Do you involve them in their children's education, in school and at home?

Then consider what you may be doing that is not consistent with whole language.

- Are you and your pupils controlled by basal readers, workbooks, textbooks, and tests?

- Do you make the choices of what your pupils will read, what they will write about, how they will go about each task you assign?

- Are all your pupils doing the same assignments, the same work sheers, the same activities much of the time? Do you lecture a lot? Do your pupils seem always to wait for you to tell them what to do?

Finally, take the first steps toward whole language.

Make decisions

Decide which strong points to expand on and which negative ones to de-emphasize. Trust that small first steps will lead to other more important ones. Move your desk into a corner to support a shift away from a teacher-dominated room. Put materials on open shelves and ask the class to set rules for getting and using them. Rearrange the seating to facilitate pupil interaction.

Confront the basics

If your program is dominated by basals, workbooks, and tests, you will need to shift away from them to authentic reading. It can happen over time. A first step may be to ensure the availability of a range of materials. Arrange with school and/or public librarians to borrow a collection of appropriate books for your room. Get your kids involved in one or more paperback book clubs. Set up a store corner in your classroom and stock it with empty boxes and containers. Build your classroom, with the kids' help, into a literate environment.

Now cut back on your use of the basal, maybe one group at a time. Your top group can easily be shifted into a personalized reading approach. If administrators or school policies require the use of basals, let the kids read through them quickly on their own, with occasional group discussions about particular selections. Then let the pupils choose their own material for sustained silent reading and develop book talks, dramatizations and other ways of sharing. Schedule individual conferences during the time you formerly met with the group.

Gradually move other pupils into a personalized, independent reading curriculum. They'll need more support, no doubt, but you'll find they are more capable of independence than you expect, and are able to read sophisticated and complex material if it's interesting to them and they choose it. Liberating your better and average readers and helping them move ahead at their own pace has an added bonus: eventually their improvement will show on standardized tests and they'll raise the class mean score. Meanwhile, you'll have the deep-down satisfaction of knowing they did it your way. You'll know also what the tests don't show: they've improved their effectiveness, efficiency, and breadth of reading. And they enjoy reading!

Diminish the use of workbooks and exercise sheets for all your pupils. Save only the few exercises that might qualify as strategy lessons, those with whole, meaningful texts that might be relevant and interesting to your pupils. Begin to develop your own strategy lessons and ways of involving all your pupils in real literacy events

- reading and writing for all kinds of purposes.

Begin developing strategy lessons for your least effective readers. The primary goal is to help them revalue themselves and the reading process. They need the most one-on-one support. They need meaningful, functional, relevant reading and writing experiences because they are the least able to deal with abstraction and because they become easily discouraged. Suitable strategy lessons will help them build the basic strategies of prediction, inference, self-monitoring, and self-correction. Gentle support and sensible materials suitable for their age and interests are what they need most of all.

Get rid of the Wombats

Virginia Ferguson, an Australian children's author and reading consultant, did a little study to find out how pupils recalled learning to read. She asked one pupil to read a book for her. "I can't. Miss. I'm only in Wombats." The Kookaburras had far greater confidence. It's clear to kids that being placed in a low group is stigmatizing, while being in a high group is an honor. Shifting toward more flexible cross-ability grouping is another way to shift toward whole language. Less able readers perk up when they realize they have much to contribute to group activities and group projects: a lot of information about some topics; ability to design and help produce displays and dioramas; a function in dramatizing stories. Insightful teachers find the strengths of all and encourage everyone to work in sharing ways.

Get writing going

Many teachers who shift to whole language find that their writing initiatives develop most rapidly. Often that's because their pupils did very little writing before. Even young children can keep journals and write every day. Establishing a classroom mailbox for notes by and for kids makes writing an integral part of your approach. Don't be too concerned that six-year-olds write anonymous nasty notes to each other. It isn't hard to redirect their energies into less anti-social functions.

It may be hard to let go of formal, textbook-based spelling and handwriting programs. But remember: misspellings are mostly confined to words being used for the first time, and punctuation is virtually impossible to teach anyway. Set yourself to watch and help pupils as they move toward conventional adult use. Keep folders of the writing kids produce and watch how their spelling and handwriting develop. Remind yourself, as well as administrators and parents, that invented spellings show development of personal rules that lead, finally, toward standard spellings.

Most whole language teachers establish special status for writing that is published, and require editing to standardize spellings. In this editing for publication they build strategies for how to identify and correct nonstandard spellings.

Children of all ages write best when they are able to choose their own topics. They don't need story starters or assigned topics. Within a thematic unit, by all means suggest a range of topics for choice, but also make it possible for kids to suggest a topic of their own.

The primary criterion for handwriting is legibility. The best way of helping children achieve greater legibility is making sure they care, because they have something to say to an audience they have chosen.

Individual conferences enable you to offer support. Or you might meet with a small group of children you think can profit from help, to deal with particular aspects of handwriting still using their own writing as the base.

Set lines of communication

As you proceed, you will want to look at the lines of communication in your classroom. Neither you nor your pupils may be totally comfortable with a sudden transition to a classroom that encourages all kinds of discussions, deliberations, and other language transactions not solely through you. Maybe kids will mistake the shift for a lack of discipline, and chaos can be the immediate result. A gradual transition, and much talk with the kids about reasons and ground rules, will be wise. Here are some steps:

- Reorganize or re-establish "sharing" time so that the kids run it with rotating chairpersons. With the kids, establish rules for who speaks when, and how to ask questions or raise criticisms in courteous and supportive ways.

- Reorganize math and other instruction so pupils are working together, and encourage them to use discussion and interaction to solve problems.

- Create small groups with very specific group tasks. Make sure the participants know what they are expected to do and have some sense of how to organize themselves to do it.

Even older pupils may not have had any experience in these things. They will need careful support and guidance until they become comfortable with the changed ground rules. The key is to involve them in thinking through and setting up the rules. Like everything else worth doing in a whole language classroom, it may take time to reach the point where there is a maximum of functional language interaction, mostly on task.

Resolve the noise problem

Teachers have traditionally abhorred noise. Next to silence, it's the hardest thing to tolerate. We want to fill silence; we want to cut down on noise. Teach yourself to stand where you can see everything and observe what the noise is, who is producing it, and how it relates to what the kids are supposed to be doing. You'll often find that most of the noise is very much related to the kind of language transactions you want. When not, move in to help re-establish purpose. Who knows, confusion may reign because you took too much for granted and didn't anticipate problems kids would have in understanding what to do or in organizing themselves. Or you may have assumed more experience, interest, or background than was justified. That requires re-planning, and then another shot at getting them on track. There is nothing wrong with reminding kids to keep noise levels down, but there's no profit in carping.

Maintain order

It's no harder to maintain order in a whole language classroom than in a teacher-dominated one. Kids involved in authentic speech and literacy events they helped to choose and plan will produce orderly activity. Whole language teachers do not abdicate control; they exercise it more subtly. The kids know who's in charge, and they know they can depend on the teacher when they need to. They know there is an order, a set of rules, and a structure in their classroom.

Teachers plan for all this and keep watch constantly. But it isn't necessary to constantly assert authority or to constantly engage in battles with the kids for control. For starters, a well-organized whole language classroom eliminates the problem of kids who have to wait for the teacher to tell them what to do next. There's always plenty to do, because the units are ongoing and because reading, writing, and discussing have their legitimate place.

Develop oral language

People learn how to converse, discuss, and listen by conversing, discussing, and listening. Kids who aren't very effective in any of these activities most likely haven't been involved in enough classroom speech events. Build a variety of ways of working in your classroom so that sometimes the kids work in twos or threes, sometimes in small groups, sometimes in larger groups, and sometimes together as a whole class. Legitimate activities will give kids opportunities to learn how to get their points across, how to plan what they want to say, what resources they need to have, and how to be understood and accepted in all kinds of interactions and presentations. Good kid-watchers monitor interactions and note how they can assist individual kids and groups in becoming more effective.

Plan

Long-range, middle-term and immediate plans should all be seen as opportunities for development toward long-term goals: expanding the pupils' language effectiveness, broadening their knowledge and conceptual base, and positively improving their attitudes toward themselves and others. Short-term plans that cover periods of days and weeks are unified by themes or units: solving real problems in science and social studies. They involve being sure that the right materials are available at the right time, reading a specific book to a group or to the class, organizing a trip to the post office to find out how the letters the kids have written to pen pals are processed. These are the ongoing activities that keep the medium and long-term plans moving. Whole language teachers also develop middle-range plans for individuals or groups: how to broaden the interests of a boy who only reads electronics catalogues, how to bring together a group of kids of mixed abilities who share an interest in computers.

Planning is a must. It means taking control back from the basal reader manuals, from the mastery-learning skill sequences, the workbooks and the test-makers. Professionals are always in control of their own work. Whole language teachers have no choice. Other professionals may be able to advise you, but your plan must be yours and must involve your pupils' participation.

It's wise to document your planning. At all times you need to be able to show administrators where you've been, where you're going, and how everything you're doing relates to your plans. You need to be able to demonstrate that you don't need the manual to tell you what your kids need.

Evaluate for self-protection

Kid-watchers know the signs of growth, of learning, of teachable moments. Teachers know how to interpret what kids do, how to see the competence and the needs that underlie what they do.

Keeping good records is part of being a good kid-watcher. Records are the stimulus to good planning, but also a matter of self-protection against unenlightened administrators who know only one way of evaluating students and teachers - standardized tests. Collect all kinds of evidence of the growth of your pupils: folders of the writing they produce over a year's time; tapes of each child reading; a series of anecdotes showing changes in work habits, in interests, in effectiveness; a record of what kids have read and how they've responded to it; photographs, videotapes; parent correspondence; analyses of performances on informal and formal tests. One of the most important kinds of evidence of the value of instruction is in the evaluations the kids are able to make of themselves. And nothing will get through to a skeptical parent like the satisfied voice of their child saying, "Now I can do it."

Form support and study groups

Whole language teaching is a grassroots movement among teachers. Deciding to take charge of your own classroom is an act of courage in an era of a shortage of jobs for teachers and a regressive back-to-basics curricular trend. It's particularly scary if you're the only teacher in your school to do so. Many teachers have formed support and study groups. They get together to cry on each other's shoulders, to engage in self-help group therapy, to share triumphs. They discuss whole language techniques, strategies, and units. They plan ways of dealing with skeptical colleagues, threatened administrators, bewildered parents. They find themselves engaged in in-service education for their colleagues, as well as for themselves. They organize presentations at conferences and plan their own public conferences and demonstrations. A loose network of such groups has developed. Some, but not all, call themselves TAWL, Teachers Applying Whole Language. Whole language newsletters are being produced. Conferences are being organized, including one in Halifax, Nova Scotia, that attracted 1500 delegates.

Bring the kids and the parents along

A whole language, child-centered, integrated approach to teaching and learning is sensible, but seems strange to people used to traditional programs. Even kids may be expecting work organized around textbooks, workbooks, and sequenced exercises. Whole language teachers need to help pupils be aware of how they learn to read and write by reading and writing, of how they become better able to use language by getting lots of opportunities to use it. Have them keep folders of their written work over a span of time, a log of their reading, tapes of themselves reading orally every so often. They'll show themselves.

Take parents along with you. They appreciate hard-working

teachers who respect their kids and who know what they're doing. Whole language involves a humanistic/scientific knowledge base, but there are no great mysteries in it. Parents can grasp the key notions. You're celebrating the language and language learning ability of their sons and daughters. You're helping their children grow while accepting who and what they are. You're treating them, their language, and their life experiences as inseparable wholes. Parents will appreciate with you a delightful invented spelling, a marvelous reading miscue, an ingenious punctuation strategy, just as they will appreciate the first sensitive attempt at poetry, a touching telling of the death of a pet, and the class-composed operatic representation of Tomie De Paola's book, *Strega Nona*.

Hold meetings with parents to explain your views of language, of learning, of teaching, and of curriculum. Suggest ways they can help and can judge their children's progress. With some support, parents can become enlightened kid-watchers too. They should be invited to visit the classroom often. When they come, help them understand what is happening and why. Parents will respond positively if they feel that teachers are professionals who really know what they are doing and genuinely care about their kids.

Don't apologize for deserting the basals and the spellers, but be prepared to help parents understand that you have better ways of helping their children develop and grow. They will become your greatest supporters and your best defense if you keep them informed and ask for their help.

Keep administrators on your side

Administrators, too, are an embattled lot these days. Many have become ardent supporters and implementers of a whole language, child-centered, integrated approach. However, many others are not well informed about language education, although they appreciate teachers who know what they are doing, who have strong commitments to their beliefs and to kids, and who are willing to take responsibility for their success or failure. Whole language teachers will need to make their plans available for review, to keep good records of activities and achievements, and to find opportunities to explain what they are doing and why they are doing it. Wise administrators will rely on effective whole language teachers to support the child-centered, integrated approach, and to bring it and the rest of the staff along.

Many whole language teachers involve their principals in the teaching and learning activities in their classrooms. They invite their principals to come in regularly to read to a group of kids. They encourage pupils to write notes to the principal that he or she will respond to. They share parent communications with the principal and make sure he or she knows when the class is doing something interesting and exciting. They encourage children to let the principal hear their reading, see their writing, and appreciate their successes.

Remind yourself and others what it's all about

One very important point for decision-makers, teacher educators, administrators, parents, and teachers themselves to remember is this: all kids are whole language learners, but there are no whole language classrooms without whole language teachers.

10

Afterword: Whole Language And The Pedagogy Of The Absurd

The success of whole language in changing the nature of education, particularly literacy education, makes it a highly visible target for political forces seeking to roll back educational change and shift education from a societal responsibility to a parental one. "It's the tall poppies that get cut down" say my Aussie friends and whole language has become a tall poppy, indeed.

Here are some comments that I made at an NCTE conference in 1991 which have proven to be prophetic.

In my workshops on whole language and in critical articles in journals people keep looking for the secret of whole language: a two word definition or a simple set of materials to plug into a conventional curriculum.

What whole language really is: Self-empowered teachers

taking the best available knowledge about language, about learners, about curriculum, about teaching and about building the learning community and turning it into reality for learners in their classrooms. It involves a body of knowledge, and a humanistic philosophy that values all learners, but it is teachers who have proclaimed themselves professionals and who have turned this all into practical reality.

If you want to understand whole language you must, more than anything understand this new professionalism among teachers.

So I thought with all due respect for Eve Merriam's text that I would begin with a variation on her parable of the Wise Woman. (In Merriam's story *The Wise Woman*, neighbors are hunting for the secret to her wisdom.)

Once there was a strange secret gathering. It was composed of a number of quite disparate groups. They had come together to try to understand a strange and powerful force which was sweeping the land: they knew it was powerful because it was shaking the foundations of the most important educational institutions in the country: the textbook publishers and the test makers. It was spreading from classroom to classroom, from school to school, from district to district, from state to state. Teachers infected by the force were exhibiting strange changes of behavior and students were engaged in really abnormal behavior: they were reading, they were writing, they were solving problems, they were asking real questions and finding their own answers.

A group of experimental researchers were the first to offer their explanations at the meeting: They had done careful meta-analyses of all the important research (that is experimental research) and had reached the unquestionably research-based conclusion that none of this could be taking place. What teachers were teaching and what learners were learning had been shown by their research to be impossible. Furthermore, said the researchers, they were outraged at the increasing frequency with which teachers were telling them that they, the mighty researchers, were irrelevant. They therefore concluded that these teachers are being deluded by evangelical gurus.

Then spake the publishers. They told tales of great upheaval: of nervous sales representatives carrying tales back from the field of teachers demanding real literature in reading text books, of refusing to use work books, of insisting on using money usually reserved for text book purchase to buy real literature for their pupils to read. The publishers had decided, they said, on a two tier response: they would capitalize on the temporary fad of using real literature which had increased the sales of kids' trade books by 500% in the previous ten years. Meanwhile they would embark on a campaign of disinformation. All their subsequent basals would henceforth be labeled whole language basals; thus they would fool the teachers into thinking that they were part of the whole language movement when they were not. Though it was too early to evaluate this strategy, reports from the field were mixed. A surprising number of teachers, it was reported, appeared able to detect phony whole language materials.

Then the school administrators spoke. The new force was becoming increasingly troublesome. There was no telling where it might break out next. It was even spreading to private and religious schools. Outbreaks had been noticed in the bible belt, in rural schools - even in the suburbs. In its worst form it disrupted usual power relationships. Teachers were being emboldened to take power - they were even taking the notion of site based management seriously and demanding real power in their classes. Even worse there were frequent reports of infiltration into the ranks of administrators. As this was uttered the administrators began to eye each other strangely. We've issued mandates, said the administrators, but we're not sure we'll be able to enforce them.

Now it was the politicians turn: There they were, governors of the states led by a former member of their group, who it was reported sat at the right hand, of the President. Not to worry they said. You folks are taking teachers far too seriously. We, politicians, have studied the educational scene in America - and we have found it to be a total failure. And we know why it has failed: the teachers and the pupils are to blame. We can solve that through a narrow national curriculum, a national test for teachers to weed out the trouble makers (and minorities) and a new test for kids. Leave it to us to leave no child, teacher or school untouched.

Writing anti-whole language into law

Strangely the greatest recognition of the soundness of whole language views of literacy and literacy education is that the so-called "Reading Wars" have been framed in the press and the speech and acts of politicians as for and against whole language. In the " Reading Wars" direct instruction of phonics and phonemic awareness are presented as research based (because they are not whole language) and the major premises of whole language are rejected as unproven or disproved though the evidence cited to support that claim does not examine any of the premises of whole language.

There have always been different views of literacy and literacy education. And of course these views do not separate easily into two mutually exclusive views. But a sustained campaign framed as for and against whole language has had two goals. One is to present a single narrow view of reading based on direct instruction of phonics as the scientifically proven alternative to whole language. And the other is to characterize anything other than this narrow approach as whole language in disguise. By doing so, not only is whole language marginalized but so is the wide range of alternate views in theory and research in the field of literacy.

To seal the victory over whole language of anti-whole language it was written into law, first in the Reading Excellence Act and then Into the No Child Left Behind revision of the Elementary and Secondary Education Act.

I've argued in other works, *In Defense of Good Teaching* and *Saving Our Schools,* that the real purpose of the attacks on whole language is to discredit public education and marginalize scientific views while replacing them with pseudo-science. In the political climate of the early 21st century, as the Union of Concerned Scientists has argued, science is being shaped to serve the political agenda of the power elite.

The NCLB law serves the political agenda: each major principle of whole language is explicitly rejected and an opposite view is given legal status.

Differences in definitions of reading

In whole language reading is construction of meaning during a transaction between the reader and the text. It is making sense of print. The federal law defines reading as rapid accurate, automatic word recognition, with meaning the by-product. While we might agree that ultimately the reader must comprehend, what comprehension is, how it is to be achieved and judged are very different.

Those different definitions lead to different views of what learning to read is and how best to help children learn to read. They lead to very different research. The law draws on a summary of reading research by the National Reading Panel that excluded any research that was not an instructional experiment designed to teach phonics and word attack. Whole language relies on a wide range of research on the reading process, reading development and reading instruction. Research methods from several foundational disciplines: linguistics, anthropology, sociology, developmental psychology, and education among others.

And the two views lead to very different evaluation. Whole language relies, to a great extent, on self-evaluation by learners and kid-watching by teachers. Tests like the Dibels, which judges reading by how many nonsense syllables a kindergarten or first grade child can sound out in one minute, are mandated in the enforcement of the law and used to classify beginners as at risk and failing.

Differences in theories of learning

In whole language, language is both a personal and social invention: human beings have the unique ability to think symbolically and to invent language both individually and socially. In this view written language is learned and develops in much the same way as oral language in the context of its functional use. The law takes the view that all learning is a response to direct instruction and there is little difference between how language is learned and how any skill is acquired. So materials for reading instruction are decodable built carefully only on skills taught out of context and sequentially. It rejects the whole language belief that learning needs to involve complete meaningful texts. In whole language, texts used in reading instruction are authentic and predictable for the learners.

Different views of teachers and teaching

Whole language treats teachers as knowledgeable professionals who know language, learning and children and know how to support literacy development building on what children know. In this view teachers are educated not trained. They are professionals who shape the instruction to fit the learners.

The law takes the direct instruction view that teachers are technicians who need to be required to teach a prescribed, mandated and scripted sequence of skills and need to be monitored to assure that they do so. In this view teachers are trained and highly controlled. They are not permitted to deviate from the precise sequence of the commercial program. The law provides for paradigm police who make sure teachers don't deviate from the scripted commercial programs.

Different views of curriculum

Whole language puts the focus on curriculum, on starting where the learners are. The curriculum builds on the language, experience, interests and culture of the learners. The curriculum is based on problem solving and inquiry. While social objectives are important, personal objectives are also important so the curriculum is flexible to suit the characteristics of the learners.

In this view, pupils learn to read in the course of reading to learn and to enjoy literature.

Federal law says materials, methods, and objectives must be standardized and highly sequenced. The curriculum is the same for all regardless of differences in learners and progress is dependent on mastery of each set of skills before progress to the next. In this view, learners learn to read before they read to learn.

The future of whole language

In the history of the world there have been many attempts to label new theories and understandings as unacceptable, illegal and even sacrilegious. But Copernicus and Galileo's view of the universe eventually triumphed over church and governmental rejection. Flat-earth views had to yield as evidence accumulated that the earth is a sphere. Evolution became accepted even though laws were written to ban teaching it.

And in the future wise men and women will look back on this period in education as that of the pedagogy of the absurd in which invalid and unworkable methods and materials were the law of the land and sound and sane pedagogy was forbidden.

In North America and in many parts of the world, whole language is surviving in the classrooms of committed, professional teachers who know what they are doing in their teaching and why it benefits their students. The laws banning whole language and mandating anti-whole language promise an absurd level of success they cannot possibly achieve while they turn classrooms into dismal unpleasant places in sharp contrast to the excitement and involvement in learning seen in whole language classrooms. Furthermore the penalties NCLB imposes on students, schools and school districts will produce a back lash among parents and state and local decision makers which will cause them to reject the law's mandates and turn back to the sane and sound alternatives.

Whether the term whole language survives as the term for what the movement has brought to education or not is not really important Education which is optimally successful with the full range of learners in all societies will ultimately require professional teachers, who respect and are respected by their pupils. Whatever we call successful teaching in the future, it will depend on the knowledge teachers have of how language processes work and are learned and how language is at the center of human thought, learning and communication.

The 1992-1993 Interviews Of Renowned Reading Scholars

Denny Taylor
Hofstra University

October, 2014

The typed-as-spoken 1992-1993 telephone interviews of renowned reading scholars on the research and teaching of Ken and Yetta Goodman were conducted at the beginning of a longitudinal ethnographic study of their lives and work. They provide a unique perspective on the emergence of whole language as an education movement that was social and democratic and having a positive impact on American society. The interviews also provide a counter narrative to the dominant discourse that was politically orchestrated to curb the enthusiasm of teachers and parents for the teacher-developed, child-centered teaching and learning initiatives that were making it much easier and more fun for children to learn to read and write.

Whole language was considered politically dangerous because it represented freedom for teachers to use their research-based understandings of the ways children learn to make equality and justice central to a child-centered curriculum.

The interviews make evident that the reading wars were manufactured to "quell the masses" and were not based on science. Reading researchers disagreed and there were many debates, as there should be in the academy. But these were not, and are not researchers who are at war with each other. On the contrary, many within the reading field who have argued and debated are now united in their concern for the direction reading instruction in schools has taken, and they stand together across paradigms and disciplines in their opposition to the high-stakes corporatization of public education.

Paper copies of these interviews were in storage for almost twenty years. Reading them now was a different experience than reading them then. It was the day the young woman asked the young man in Central Park if he had heard that we are "post-future", and I thought as I read these interviews, "It is true".

It is not that people have forgotten, or that their memories have failed them. Many of the teachers in our schools and many parents of public school children were taught to read and write post-NCLB. They don't remember because they have no experiences of any teaching and learning that even comes close to a child-centered whole language curriculum.

All that is left is the political propaganda, some of which reflects the disinformation coming from the White House and is promulgated by the media. Except, of course, there are the authentic accounts from the reading researchers who precede the "end of the future", who were doing the research that was so forcibly coopted for political purposes. They argued with each other, but were benevolent in their relationships with one another, and at all times did their best to maintain a collective sensibility in the best interests of children and an ethos of caring for every child.

Ken and Yetta Goodman
University of Arizona

March 14, 1993

Ken: I think the impressions that people have of us are very interesting.

Yetta: There is a tendency for people to see no difference and to confuse our work. We get asked to autograph each other's books. I find that strange.

Ken: I think our students and CELT (Center for the Expansion of Language and Thinking) can separate us. But other people can't see the difference.

Yetta: I think we both feel that we represent a continuous study group for ourselves.

Ken: Doing keynotes together puts the biggest strain on our relationship. We prepare very differently. Yetta has everything together and I am often writing notes just before I present.

Yetta: It seems to me that we do a one two punch. Ken says things that I couldn't say and I can come in with things that he might not be able to say.

Ken: Our personalities are different but we are always consistent. In Detroit in school meetings we would be tarred with the same brush. We would be called honkies and things like that, but we never took the bait and always after meetings people would come up to us and ask, "How are the kids?"

Yetta: We are often asked to do keynotes together and it is very unproductive.

Ken: In a very broad sense neither of us would have achieved so much if we had not been together. When we travel together, I am always more relaxed. When we do workshops we share the energy. And we do things that I would no longer take on.

Yetta: We have one problem, that if someone asks a question we both answer.

Ken: We've reached an agreement that only one of will answer, but it never works out that way.

Ken: One of the things you should talk about with our students some of them have difficulty deciding which one of us to work with.

Yetta: I am outwardly more accepting, and then people over time come to be just as comfortable with Ken.

Ken: I have a very strong feeling that people are selective in their reading. I don't know whether Jeanne (Chall) has read any of our work. We get quoted in ways that make me think some researchers who respond to our work haven't read us.

Yetta: Jeanne's work is on early literacy but she knows nothing about my work. Part of the problem is that there is so much work out there that we have to be selective, and then there is a tendency that we don't read the people whose work is so contradictory to our own.

Yetta: None of them acknowledge that literacy is a cultural phenomenon.

Ken: The camp work gave us a social worker view of education.

Yetta: We learned of the power of the group. Campers never had to be good or bad based on a paper and pencil test. It's a much different interaction pattern than you see in school. Not all kids are good at kickball, some kids are good at hiking. You get that perspective. You would never have homogeneous groupings in kickball for example and a lot of that came into our teaching.

Ken: And progressive education was still alive in California schools. We started a counselors' union. Did I tell you that? We worked for two years and thought that we were being exploited and so we started the union.

Yetta: Ken was president and I was secretary and in the constitution we had it that no administrators could be part of the union and in the third year we were administrators and we could no longer belong.

Yetta: I think the most important thing is that the generation of ideas depends on the community. There's often a lack of cohesion within people's work.

Ken: That comes back to your view of research, that it is okay to do the work whatever is funded.

Yetta: I've come to the point that in the academic world, so called "real" research has become an academic exercise. You find a topic and then you have to keep writing for promotion and tenure. So they are just topics.

Ken: So the fact that our research reflects our values and philosophy and our social point of view - I couldn't do it any other way.

Yetta: If you have cohesion in your research you have an opportunity to build interests and a shared belief system.

(We talk about the researchers that I interviewed, renowned scholars who worked with Ken and Yetta, students who studied with them, and who are now professors scattered across the US and in universities around the world.)

Yetta: I think the future is in good hands.

Ken: Agreed.

Harold and Betty Rosen
London Institute of Education

September 18, 1993

Harold:

Well where to start. I realize I've known Ken and Yetta for a good while. It must have been the late seventies. They are incredibly complementary.

And when I encountered them there was instant rapport. I think it was because they came from a tradition and culture that was very similar to my own.

I think what it amounts to is a very great powerful thing called radical Jewish, the whole secular culture, it is instantly recognizable in Ken and Yetta. The way they go about things. They are huge doers. And that is what I have admiration for. They make things happen, as well as being international researchers.

And it is something coming out of the style that I was talking about, and this takes a considerable amount of shrewd courage.

Coming to my department at the London Institute of Education, it was odd for them to find a department like mine. It was inspiring for them to meet so many radical teachers. They were so good at communicating with them.

In the U.S. something was needed to distinguish language from the segmentation of language, and from the beginning whole language was an inspired idea. It is very easy for teachers who teach grammar to assume that children will write more grammatically. In practice it is very easy to separate grammar from reading and writing.

I have been to several Whole Language conferences. I've been to one in Indiana, and it was very clear to me when I saw in action the networking that teachers are doing, and that it is very important.

It was interesting to see the other speakers encouraging teachers to think more deeply and more radically.

And Ken and Yetta were there, giving other people the confidence to go on and they refused to be the center of attention. It is so easy to become cult figures, but because their philosophical politics are so good they don't let this happen.

One little episode I want to share is about Ken's presidential speech at IRA and his political judgment. I remember saying to Ken if you could get all these people into a demonstration on the street it would be impressive. And it was a time when Reagan was making an attack on social services. Educational programs were being cut and Ken said in his presidential address, "If you up the armaments bill, you down the education bill." And when you think of IRA and that gathering, he was taking a calculated risk in politicizing what is usually an innocuous speech.

Betty:

Until I actually met them I came into the category of thousands and thousands of teachers who were thankful for miscue. That is my first debt to the Goodmans.

I just want to add I agree with what Harold said, that it is very easy for English teachers who teach grammar to assume that children would write more grammatically. Teaching grammar does not necessarily make children better readers and writers.

The first time I saw them they were in Sydney, and it was the first time I had seen two people giving a duel lecture, and what struck me was the ease with which they did it, and it just seemed the proper way of giving a lecture. And it applied a type of collaboration that you rarely see.

My second encounter – I don't know where we were – it was in somebody's home and eventually Yetta brought out her guitar and the way she played and sang was a total joy and she was just so relaxed and lovely and everybody was. And I remember her looking at me and it was just fleeting glances and smiles that encouraged me to join in –and it was the essence of a good primary teacher encouraging children to join in.

And my husband said, "Why don't you sing something from Wales?" And Yetta came over and I don't know what she said, but it was the way she approached me that said, "Join in" and "That's great" and "If you don't want to that's fine."

Harold:

I would like people to know something about how Ken and Yetta enter the world and how they react to the world at the same time, so that everyone can get a theoretical come practical understanding of where they stand professionally as well as personally.

Frank Smith
University of Victoria, Canada

November 30, 1992

I find every time I think I have a new idea the Goodman's seem to be involved. We got interested in writing about the same time, in spelling, and now mathematics. Ken said he was starting to work with a neurologist. I said I thought neurologists had a lot to shed on learning.

I have always been particularly influenced by Yetta. I got very involved with the environment of the classroom. Not what teachers should do but in the environment. Ken has always impressed me with his political acumen as well as his theoretical. I think it's from Yetta that I have this feeling that it all comes down to individual teachers and individual children, and I give enormous credit to Yetta for her kid-watching.

I've been looking at old theses from the twenties. I think whatever is going on was going on for centuries. I don't think any new arguments came up. We were all really saying that there hadn't been any advances since Huey.

The first thing that was going on was a reaction to behaviorism which got an enormous boost in 1950's because of Sputnik. An enormous effort was made to lift American education by its bootstraps and it was going to be done by logistics, by breaking things down into little bits. It brought in massive amounts of resources to essentially produce phonics kinds of things. Time and motion people could only handle phonics. It became an incredibly mechanistic approach that was dominated by people that had a stimulus-response approach theory.

Skinner brought out his massive technical book, which was called *Contingencies of Reinforcement: A Theoretical Analysis*. His view was that everything was controlled by schedules of reinforcement and environmental stimulus responses. Mastery learning, phonics instruction, short words, short sentences, lots of testing. Lots of curriculum development was done by teachers but it was done by prescriptions laid down for them. Twenty regional labs were established in the 1960's.

They were called Regional Laboratories for Educational Research and Development. I worked for one of them in 1967 and eventually left. I couldn't understand what they were doing. It was a factory for fill-in-the-blank activities for children. Enormous amounts of money, much more money than is introduced today, and all sorts of people were funded who knew nothing about teaching but knew a lot about systems analysis. Educators were working with NASA.

I got my degree in visual perception at Harvard. The research that I did demonstrated that people could recognize whole words as easily as five letters. People could recognize entire words in the amount of time it took them to read individual letters. Back in that time before I even got into education it occurred to me that people could not be reading individual letters when they read words.

I was writing about language in Australia. Chomsky was

important at that time. The person I read was George Miller, who interpreted Chomsky for psychologists. Miller argued that language was a creative constructive process that ran on meaning. Just before that time Chomsky had produced his own paper that savaged Skinner. They argued that behaviorism was dead. Miller said they had done some experiments and had come to the conclusion that "mind" was more than just a four letter word.

Now you see in the early 1960's I had left Australia to study with Miller. The point is here were a whole lot of people responding to each other. It was Chomsky's notion that language is generative and hinged on meaning that set all of us off in all kinds of directions.

The first time I met Miller at Harvard, Chomsky was in his office. He was looking very casual, I thought he was a brother-in-law or a painter. I just spent all my time talking to Miller about language and creativity. But I think this was typical. I think Miller deserves great credit for making Chomsky accessible. Miller and Bruner with enormous help from Chomsky set up the Center for Cognitive Science at Harvard, and it was there that psycholinguistics was born. I spent a year at Cornell in 66/67 on something called Project Literacy with Harry Levin and Eleanor Gibson. Eleanor Duckworth, Paul Kohler and, I think, Roger Shuy was involved. I was actually finishing off my research. Then I went to the South West Regional Laboratory. Some of them are still in existence and they are still producing the same materials.

Now we get to the bit of my history that is relevant. From California I came up to Canada in April 1969. I had a job opportunity the year before and turned it down but decided to go a year later. The job I got was at OISE. I was put in the curriculum department and the job I was given was to teach reading. I had never done that before in my life. I had never taken a course on education and I had never taught teachers. The teachers I was working with were graduates, incredibly knowledgeable people, I was intimidated by them.

When I went to the library I found shelves of books on teaching reading but no books on reading. So I went back to my group and told them my dilemma and what I was going to do with their help was to try to understand what goes on when a kid learns to read. It is very difficult to get teachers to see the difference between teaching and learning. Very quickly I wrote *Understanding Reading*, which was essentially my course notes, which was my analysis of learning to read from a psycholinguistic sociological perspective. Which leads to the question what exactly is learning? I called it psycholinguistics and dedicated it to George Miller. I made it quite clear I was not telling teachers how to teach reading, which seems to me to be counterproductive. It has nothing to do with procedures or techniques.

Although *Understanding Reading* was a highly technical book, the message was you have to sort this out for yourself, don't let any expert tell you how to teach reading. Now I sent that off to my publisher, I was supposed to be writing a language book. The publisher sent it out to Paul Kohler. He was profoundly influential in those days. He was at Toronto at the time. He was one of the reviewers. Harold Shane was another. He was at least as influential as Roger Shuy. We have to recognize that things were stirring in sociology with people like Labov. The third reviewer was Kenneth Goodman, who I had never heard of and he had never heard of me. What I do know is that all three reviewers wrote encouraging reviews and the book came out in 1971.

Now in 1970 I went to my first IRA in Anaheim and it was particularly mind-boggling. I had just gone out of curiosity. And as I remember I had been there for about three days when a mob of what I thought were totally manic young people grabbed me and said I had to come and meet Ken Goodman. Which immediately turned me off. I was saying, "Who is Ken Goodman?" and I was told that Ken had seen my book.

I met Ken and Yetta and, of course, I was tremendously comfortable with them. They were very supportive, even though we came from totally different perspectives. Ken and I hit it off so well I thought we should consummate our meeting by publishing an article together. The article, "On the Psycholinguistic Method of Teaching Reading", came out in January 1971 in *Elementary School Journal*. It is the only thing I have ever published with Ken.

In the article we argued that there is no such thing as a "psycholinguistic method" of teaching reading and we said the approach was not a method. It was a preemptive article and of course we failed completely. People were asking everywhere, "How do I teach using a psycholinguistic method?"

Ever since then Ken and Yetta and I have gone on different paths. The people I met during the first year or two, probably fifteen, twenty people, became my friends, and they were the core of whole language, they stimulate me, but I've never joined them. I have always been very inspired by the people who work with Ken and Yetta without becoming myself a part of the movement.

It is difficult to focus on Ken without focusing on Yetta. It's the two of them together. They have had some brilliant ideas like miscue analysis, which has been abused in formal assessment. The moment the work they do gets formalized it gets misused. It's their ideas that are important.

In a sense my admiration is for their political acumen. Education does not just take place in classrooms, it is a political situation. I also think their work in bilingual education is important. In a sense they introduced me to bilingual conferences. Their social awareness and social sensitivity are very important.

Brian Cambourne
University of Wollongong, Australia

January 31, 1993

I first became aware of Ken's work when I was a professor in Australia teaching in a little teachers' college in Wagga Wagga. I read an article called "Let's Dump the Uptight Model in English" and it came at a time when I had been given the job of running courses in reading and writing. Back then they were taught separately. My background in reading was fairly traditional, but I had done a lot of research into kid's language and, because I was given the responsibility of developing a curriculum, I was reading as widely as I could and I was dissatisfied with what I was reading.

I had read Chall's stuff and all the articles in the *Reading Teacher* and the *Reading Research Quarterly* for a three or four year period. I think it was because I had done a qualitative doctoral dissertation and everything I was reading was quantitative that I distrusted what the articles were saying.

When I read Ken's article it resonated with the dissatisfaction I was feeling. And from that article I went on to one written by Yetta on miscue and from that point on I just grabbed anything I could by the Goodmans. I taught myself miscue and I guess I became enthusiastic in my own country at looking at reading as language.

In one of his articles Ken made the statement that it was all language, reading included. All of the literature I was reading implicitly treated reading as a different form of language, and Ken's statement, "It's all language", helped me put the big picture together. And it was at that time that Peter Rausch arrived at Wagga Wagga as my Dean, and when he walked into my office he saw Goodman's work all over the place, and he asked me if I liked Ken's work and then he told me he had just got back from working with Ken at Wayne State. Peter and I became good friends and I was able to learn miscue from an insider.

It was at that time that I took a sabbatical and did a post doc. Courtney Cazden was an outside reader on my dissertation committee and she invited me to study at Harvard. And it was there I was put in the Harvard School of Education with Jeanne Chall and Courtney Cazden and Carol Chomsky.

I had cross registration privileges at MIT and I spent a lot of time with the people in artificial intelligence, people like Marvin Minsky. And I could see all these bright young people doing graduate work through Harvard never studying the work that Ken was doing, and I challenged Jeanne Chall. I told her I'm going to write a paper and analyze Ken's work and she said that was a good idea and it was at that time I became aware of the intensity of feelings simmering below the surface of the "Great Debate" in the reading field in America. I became aware of the way in which people protect their own turf.

While I was researching Goodman I decided to go and talk with him, so I phoned Ken and I asked him how far it was to Detroit and he said, "Oh not far", and so I took a bus, and I spent two weeks living with Ken and Yetta in their house. And I met Dorothy Watson and Dorothy Menosky and everyone else at the Miscue Center.

And it was there that Ken gave me a study that he was finishing on the analysis of kids from different linguistic groups in America. I told him I was going to audit the paper and I don't think he knew what I meant. I said I was going to work through his data from the back, and just see if I could check the logic of his taxonomy, and it all stood up and that's where that article originally came from.

I made a bond with Ken and Yetta immediately. They had a knack of making you feel at home. They weren't threatened when you questioned them, unlike people at Harvard where Jeanne Chall and her students were terribly protective of their work. Ken would listen to the questions that I asked him, and I would try to find problems with his thinking, and he always responded in ways that were comfortable. That was opposite of people like Jeanne Chall.

I think that it is Ken. He doesn't see himself in competition with anyone, and I have found that with Ken and all his students they are driven by the same motivation. It is about making learning to read barrier free. And somehow it rubs off on the students that he works with, and it rubs off on his other colleagues, and I think it is because there are a lot of kids out there who are being screwed up, and we want to get rid of the barrier, and that it is very different from the other professionals that I have encountered at IRA, and at other conferences in the US.

And I admire Ken and Yetta for keeping their dignity given the things people have written and said about them. I think I have only seen Ken angry once in Australia, when one of the genre people challenged him on his understanding of black kids in America. And Ken was really angry. He handled questions from these researchers by saying he was not going to make the mistake of slipping into their genre and could they put their concerns into a general framework.

I've traveled a lot with Ken. In 1980 I spent three months at the Illinois Center for the Study of Reading. Then I went to the University of Arizona in Tucson and again the treatment was different. In Illinois I was never asked to give a seminar or talk with students. In Arizona Ken asked me to run a course on qualitative research and at the end of the time he gave me $1,500 and I asked him what it was for. He said, "It's your pay for teaching the course."

Ken was responsible in Australia for turning the reading curriculum around. There was a huge change in the way we taught reading, and we brought Ken and Yetta out to Australia on a number of occasions, and Frank Smith, because between them they were turning reading instruction on its head.

They usually visited New Zealand on their way through there and offered support to Don Holdaway and Marie Clay. During the eighties New Zealand got ratings on cross cultural studies that showed that New Zealand kids were the most literate in the world. I'm not expecting the same ratings over the next few years. I'm pessimistic for Australia and about what's happening in the US.

Jeanne Chall
Harvard University

February 9, 1993

Kenneth Goodman was a younger person when I was quite well known and active in the field. He came to me with a study he had done and he said, "I want you to have this", which I thought was very nice that a younger person would come to me. This was at a meeting at the IRA. I think I read it, although I can't remember what the study was about.

And then during the sixties there was a committee formed for Project Literacy at Cornell and I was on the steering committee. Harry Levin was also on the committee. At any rate they were asking for younger people to be recommended, for people to come for a summer workshop on linguistics with basic researchers in the field and I recommended Ken. He tells the story himself, he says that I got him into "the big time".

I didn't meet Yetta until much later. I was not at the summer institute. After that time I used to meet him at conferences. I had a nephew who lived in Tucson and I called them when I was visiting and they invited me to their house. They were very gracious. They were also nice to a former student of mine.

And then, being the Director of the Reading Lab at Harvard, there was an NCTE meeting in Boston, and we had a special seminar for Ken and Yetta, and they spoke about their "psycholinguistic guessing game". Well one of the things that I think is quite characteristic of him and disappointing of him was that the students came over and said to me, "Well if he is right, we're not right," and I went over to him and said, "Why don't we do a study? We can select classes in kindergarten and first grade and study them longitudinally. You do it your way and we'll do it our way. All we have to agree on is the tests."

And he said, "Tests? I don't believe in tests." So that made it impossible for us to do the study. Unfortunately from the very start he never paid attention to results. He doesn't talk research evidence and he says, "I've got research" and I say "but I haven't seen it".

I think unfortunately he is paying for it now. I think he has a following among unsophisticated people but not sophisticated researchers, which must hurt him in some way.

I think he found another rather more complex way to measure errors. He never specified level of difficulty in relation to a child's reading level. It was never clear. It was so open you could do anything you wanted. I think it pretty much confirmed what other people have found since, miscue is a technique, a tool, but it is not a theory.

You see almost every major person has done some work on tests, comprehension, beginning reading, reading difficulties. I have never seen miscue as part of his theory. Let's take one of his ideas, which is a central idea in his work, teacher empowerment. What has that to do with miscue analysis? Or, being against direct instruction? Basal readers? Phonics instruction?

I really benefitted from the IRA debate I had with him. I have made many new friends because of it. We are very good friends and we would basically never do anything to hurt each other.

He has every right to do what he wants to do, but I had just hoped that we would have done some collaborative research. Basically I don't think he has contributed very much. Miscue is not basic research. You see, just because students make certain a kind of errors doesn't mean you teach to those errors.

His main contribution is freedom for teachers.

Miscue is just like economics, its laissez faire economics and it doesn't work. People are starving you have to have some welfare. If you look at the end part of my book *Learning to Read: The Great Debate*, you will see there is the recommendation that teachers have the freedom to teach as long as the children are producing. This whole idea of freeing teachers was not discovered with whole language. But you must be judged by results. Everyone is judged by results.

I like them very much and I think they feel the same way towards me and I treated him the same way as I would my own child. I thought he had ability and I supported him. I have never come out directly against him.

We are really only doing this so that the children do better and the teachers do better at teaching them. Some things make it difficult to settle some of this. The findings of the dissertations that I have read is that whole language is better in kindergarten and first grade but by third and fourth grade children need phonics and direct instruction. I don't know why Ken has not done research and why he hasn't read the research of others.

In qualitative research they don't talk about what is important. How well the children are reading and writing. Not just that they are reading well in the early grades but how do they do in the middle grades.

If Ken and Yetta collected data over ten years, suppose the children do fall in third and fourth grade but that they do catch up and you find that by college freshmen they write creatively etc. then we'll know that whole language works. He promises this but he doesn't show this. There are no studies to support his position.

It saddens me that someone who is that bright and has that kind of understandings could throw out all structure. I think he is too smart to know what it is about. I would like to know their motivations. Something more about them as people. Particularly him. What was it in his learning experiences that got him to go in this direction? I really expect more of him. I am a little bit motherly towards him. I recognized his ability very early. I just hoped he would do more.

Richard Anderson
University of Illinois

March 11, 1993

Well I wouldn't count the Goodmans as close friends. I have known them for about twenty years. They have been personally cordial to me and we have had good times now and then. In Australia I spent a weekend on the Great Barrier Reef with them. We've had a lot of perspectives in common, but I think Ken in public emphasizes the points on which we disagree rather than the points on which we agree. I think he feels it necessary to maintain his position publicly at all times. I think that there is no doubting the substantial influence of the Goodmans.

The whole language movement has to be counted as a popular success in winning the minds and hearts of teachers – certainly belief in the power and value of involvement, natural involvement in written language. I suppose I have also had some nervousness about direct instruction. Ken would probably see that as a difference and I think it's true that he would seldom find any time for direct instruction, and I am more eclectic on that point. I am more of an empiricist than Ken. I have seen people reach all kinds of conclusions by what they see as self-evident or self-truths, and I guess I am more impressed by the complexity of language and would like to see more proof of the pudding.

One way I see Ken is as a born again progressive educator as much in the steps of John Dewey as much as anyone in the field. That may not reflect his formative experiences, but I would like some kind of inside view that would allow me to understand what teachers of his history and social experience – what caused him to be the sort of person that he is. I think Ken has held on to a certain position and I think it is his staying power that has led to his success. Sometimes he is intransigent.

Phil Gough has debated with Ken a couple of times and has been pretty resolute in holding to a different view. In my case it is my eclecticism that annoys Ken, whereas for people like Jeanne Chall and Phil Gough the issue of direct instructions and phonics.

Carolyn Burke
Indiana University

June 5, 1993

Well I was teaching in Highland Park public schools. I taught first grade and readiness. In 1965 I was working on my masters at Wayne. I was working on my thesis and I went into the office of my adviser and found out he had left the university, and Brooks Smith was the Chair of the Department, he asked me if I had taken a course in Linguistics.

It's funny the way advisors talk like that. All I wanted to do was finish.

Brooks was an important part of our experience. He and Ken worked together and shared a vision of education. He was Ken's mentor and he was a cornerstone for all of us.

And one of the courses I ended up taking was Ken Goodman's. I only realized later that it was a doctoral seminar. Ken had already done his pilot study in miscue and he had started using the word "miscue" in his research, and he asked me if I had thought of doing a doctorate, and that threw me for a loop.

Yetta was working on her doctorate at the time and she was looking for students for her dissertation research. My kids were part of that study. There could have been some other students in Thompson school, but it was my kids, my little Jeffrey, who turned out to be so interesting.

One of the other things that I remember is Yetta and I making a presentation to the education faculty, sharing the early miscue research. We did it purposefully to keep them informed and invite them in. Ken was making everyone very nervous, and he decided it would be better if Yetta and I did it.

The overriding concern was dialect and we got critiques from everyone about that, and they said it was a problem with our research, and we said these are children in our schools, and we said that we needed to understand reading for every student. They were concerned that miscue was laissez faire and we would let kids go through school and they wouldn't be prepared for the workplace. And we were surprised at how strong the feelings were and so we had an open house twice a year and we would invite faculty and students to try to make sure that we didn't alienate them.

One of the earliest consultants was Ron Wardhaugh. Each of us would code a particular student and it would sometimes take you up to a week to code one reading for a kid, so we saved our questions and we developed a procedure of plodding ahead and you made your best decision and circled it, and then on Friday the whole day was spent around the table looking at questionable codings and some of the codings would change.

Every time you made a new decision based on a new perspective, you had to go back through all of the stories that were coded. Fridays were really exciting times, that was when all the new discoveries were solidified. We looked forward to Fridays. We were starting to get a number of miscues that, even though we were consistent, the explanations were complicated, so we started inviting linguists in, and Ron Wardhaugh was the first. All the linguists thought there was no link between their work and what we were doing, but Ron came and we had about 98 examples of miscues and we read off our miscues and he said, "Hmm, that's really interesting," and we read them off, and he kept saying that. He said, "You know, what you don't know, linguists don't know either."

We were flabbergasted. Then we had to sit back and say, "Well there is something new about language that we are discovering here."

Frank Smith was one of the people who consulted. For several years Frank was large in our lives. Frank and I think Ken were worried that as we focused on instruction, we would make students self-conscious of the language processes they were using and it would inhibit their learning. Frank Smith actually made public presentations about it.

And we said, "You're wrong. You know a lot about language but not about teaching."

Ken and I made a presentation in California for CELT (Center for the Expansion of Language and Thinking). We were both making keynote addresses and my presentation centered on the questions I ask readers. Readers from a very young age are implementing a theoretical perspective of language and they are very consistent in their use.

And Ken started by saying, "First I have to make a public apology to Carolyn and Yetta. I have been arguing with Carolyn and Yetta about making the reader self-conscious and I was wrong."

That was important for me. Arguing with Frank didn't make me nervous, but it made me very nervous to have Ken questioning me, that was a very different.

From the point of view of how these little groups have formed. One way to trace these activities is to trace the groups.

SALE (Seminar in Applied Linguistics Education) started at Wayne State. One of the things that was interesting was that Ken started pulling students from University of Michigan, who would come down to spend a day with us at the Miscue Center, and we began to realize that we needed was an organization for ourselves. At that time we were doing an awful amount of travel. Conferences, workshops, and Ken taught a course at Ohio State and he had to fly in.

SALE was started to help us sit back and think about the theories that we were building. The move from SALE to CELT came as a way to help students who had finished their degrees and left to stay connected.

Then there's TAWL (Teachers Applying Whole Language) and the Whole Language Umbrella. I always attribute the first notion of TAWL to Dorothy Watson. She said, "I've got all these students out here" and she formally started pulling classroom teachers together. I think TAWL was her invention, she named the group. In my mind this is a whole series of organizations. We have always created these organizations to support ourselves and our colleagues.

One of the other things that is related, I know we have generated hostility and people seem to think of us as a cliquish group. I feel like a member of a multigenerational family that started at Wayne State. Jerry Harste and I talk about our students, and we ask each other which generation they are, and people look at this and they find it disturbing. They see in education isolated scholars, and the idea of participation and collaboration is so much a part of what Ken has created within the field.

I think that is what is not fully understood in education, what theoretical beliefs mean, and what "learning is social" means. One of the things that is important is that Ken is still surrounded by all his students and that is so important. Right from the beginning you are a colleague, I was so shocked when I left the Miscue Center.

One of the things I learned earliest from Ken was that whenever he had a doctoral student in his office for a conference, and I always used to vacate his office and he would say, "No, stay". And there were so many student conferences that went well, but some students would hum and ha, and they made me nervous.

Finally Ken said to me, "You cannot help someone who is not already thinking something."

And I learned that if you want help from Ken you have to have an idea. You have to think and say something and then there is an outpouring. He wouldn't tell you anything unless you tell him something first. That was an important lesson you have to share. My first real understanding of the word collaboration was what made Fridays so important, because we learned that if we were ready to take risks, we would discover something powerful and new. That's Ken's premise again, that you've got to commit yourself and you've got to take risks. Ken would be off drawing models and writing for days based on these Friday meetings. That is very much an aspect of Ken, that he understands the importance of his colleagues and collaboration.

Dorothy Menosky
New Jersey City University

October 26, 1992

I had never heard of their work. I hadn't the foggiest idea that they existed. I was just a good teacher. I had been teaching overseas and I came back and got into this school where Carolyn Burke was, and Carolyn asked if a researcher could come in and do research. And it was Yetta.

And Carolyn and I would argue. We were the only ones that came early to school and we would have a wonderful time. And we would argue about word lists and phonics and I would think I had won the argument, and she would come in the next day and whip me and I would ask how could she know that, and she was taking a course with Ken so I was surrounded by them before I ever knew them.

I went to see him. He was introducing John Goodlad and I didn't know who was who and that was my first view of him. And I signed up for a course and I immediately became schizophrenic. He was teaching us one way, and in the other course I was being taught another. He drove me crazy because he would never give us the answer and he would never tell us.

I didn't know that Ken and Yetta were married. I didn't know their work. I didn't know about any of that except what Carolyn would tell us.

Yetta would come in and do language experience in my classroom. So I decided one year that I would prove them wrong. I decided one September that I would teach my class their way and I was convinced that by December the children would not be able to read. So I abandoned my word lists and phonics and it worked! And it was very confusing because I had to dump everything that I had been doing for a number of years.

And at the end of that year Ken phoned me up and he said he had gotten his miscue research grant and would I like to be one of his research assistants. And I asked, "When do you have to know?" and he said, "Now," and I said, "Okay," and Carolyn came too.

So that's where I started, in an office that was supposed to be for one person, and Ken and Carolyn were sharing the office, and they crammed in another desk for me.

I tell you another interesting thing. When you are a student of his there comes a day when he decides that you are ready and he sends you off to do a workshop. He has never had a workshop where a student messed up.

I was scared to death the whole time. I was sure that I would do everything wrong, but he has the uncanny knack of knowing when you are ready. He did that with articles. He got called to write one by *Instructor Magazine*. He told them he didn't have time to do it. He said, "Write it," and he went over it and had the last word. He had them send me the check for 100 dollars. It was a really good deal, because it was a reprint article. He knew what you could do and what you couldn't.

A lot of things went on in the miscue center. We were doing the miscues where you had to code everything and we had to work in pencil, and we had electric pencil sharpeners, and one of the reasons was Ken and Carolyn would get together and have a meeting, and they would call us in and they would change things.

"I'm not erasing one of those," I would say. And they would say we had to. And I would say, "Well if we change this then we have to change that," and they would say, "Yes we know."

Carolyn said they would discuss who was going to tell me.

I snuck something in my dissertation in chapter two. I was talking about subvocalizing and the people I'm quoting said, "If you are not sure if they are subvocalizing you should go up and put your hands on the side of the throat." And I added, "You can cure them by squeezing." Nobody saw it and it went through.

You know when you did your defense we always had it in our conference room and everybody else was on the other side. I had such a good time during my defense. I enjoyed every minute of it. Ken makes you feel, you wrote it, it's your research, nobody knows it better than you. I had a wonderful time. Then I had to step outside and when Ken opened the door he said, "Congratulations doctor," and it was so exciting. I'm sure he still does that. And when I went back in the room everybody was smiling.

We really were just like a family. We fought, but at the same time we were very close. Everyone had their own unique way of coding. Bill Page used to have his coding sheets propped up on three great big pieces of cardboard and we wondered how he could do it like that.

We had great miscue conferences, and our very first button said,

"Miscue". You know what the trouble was? We had to leave. Wayne State would not hire its graduates so we all had to go off and get jobs and I can remember coming back for more miscue studies.

I love to watch when they are talking about education, and I love the way that Ken is so proud of Yetta being the Regents Professor. I see them touching more. I hope somehow their warmth comes through. I don't care how great they are, they never act like a big deal, ever.

Miscue was at the time of the moonwalk and the Vietnam War, and we all marched down Woodward Avenue, in Detroit. All of us, our whole campus marched. Ken and Yetta marched, Dorothy, Carolyn. We were "Teacher Educators Against the War." I wish we had "Miscueteers Against War".

Dorothy Watson
University of Missouri Kansas City

June 17, 1992

I jotted down some things. Maybe we should start with some reminiscences at Wayne State. I worked with Ken before I worked with Yetta. He got a very large grant for the study of the reading process, and he set up the reading miscue research center right off the campus at an old hotel. We had a big suite there. Carolyn Burke, Rudine Sims Bishop, Bill Page, Peter Rausch, Dorothy Menosky, Dave Allen, who was killed in an accident, were all doctoral students.

Well anyway this office was a huge suite and we had one large area where all the doctoral students worked. We had our little headsets and tape recorders. Ken looked at grades 2, 4, 6, 8, and 10, and he looked at Appalachian kids, and Samoan and Down East Maine, Navajo, inner city Detroit, Texas ranch kids who combined English and Spanish, and kids from Port Gibson, Mississippi.

We taped these kids in these grades and brought the tapes back and did the miscue analysis on them. I remember we were in this huge conference room that was a real workroom for us. We had this huge computer that we called LURCH. This room was our lunch room and our work room. Every week we would meet with Ken to negotiate and reconcile these miscues. It was a real marvelous experience. We would bring in these miscues that we couldn't figure out.

Ken said, "If we are smart enough we'll be able to figure out what kids were doing."

It was at this time that I decided not to call any kid a lazy reader, there were reasons why they did the things they did. We also had our dissertation defenses in that room, and in the other room they would be putting the wine glasses out. You could hear them preparing the celebration, so nobody ever failed a defense.

I met Yetta at IRA in Anaheim before I went to Wayne. Dave Allen introduced me to her. I just talked to her briefly at that time. I kind of remember her rushing in and rushing out. I remember the first time I saw Yetta teach. I remember that people said Ken was so low key it was hard to hold on to what he said. But she was a really marvelous teacher and I think Ken has learned to teach through Yetta.

In the suite of rooms Ken had an office but he liked to be out with the rest of us. The room was a real gathering place. We worked in the day and met there at night. SALE was the predecessor of CELT. Some of the teachers from Ann Arbor and the doctoral students and teachers from Dearborn where Yetta was teaching would come over. I think the idea got translated into CELT. Then of course Ken and Yetta started CELT. Ken was the first president and Yetta was the second. The first members of CELT were Ken, Yetta, Carolyn, Rudine, me and Dave Allen.

I have to tell you one story about the Miscue Center. Ken had this huge grant but it all went through Wayne State. I'm not sure what the snafu was but we couldn't get anyone to clean up the place. We had a woman who cleaned for us and Ken was trying to get a line item in the budget to hire her. It had to be a company so he created Ken's Careful Cleaning Company so he could hire her and he got it through alright.

We began to have workshops on miscue analysis. Everybody there was interested in curriculum. But at that time the workshops were about the reading process. How do children learn to read and what does that say about the teaching of reading? The Miscue Center was consuming.

Yetta seemed to always be - I'm thinking about Marian Edmonds who retired. Yetta arranged a love-in for her. They always had dinners and Ken would do a lot of the cooking.

Ken was President of the Faculty Council. He wanted his term to be known for what he called, "good humor and brevity", so he would manage to tell a story from the Miscue Center at the faculty meetings, but unless you had the background the stories were not always that funny. So we would go and laugh at the faculty not laughing. It was grim. We would say if this is the way faculty meetings go, then we don't want to be on the faculty. But looking back they were really typical.

Let me talk about CELT. That group has always been small. Made up of like-minded folks it's grown from miscue analysis to teacher education. For our rejuvenation conferences Ken and Yetta brought into CELT researchers like Michael Halliday, Harold Rosen, and Don Graves. Ken and Yetta seemed to be able to recognize the importance of their work before they became well known. I keep wanting to talk more of CELT, because although that organization is small it is powerful in the projects that it has done. The way it honors teachers.

Miscue is so clearly the type of research that informs teachers, you don't feel you are standing at arm's length. It is so compelling. When I started with miscue I would say I knew that all along, but Ken articulated this. I remember the very first article he wrote in Elementary English, it was a 67 article, "Reading Cues and Miscues", something like that. I remember reading it. There were three things that he said in that article. One was that kids could read more proficiently when they had contextual language rather than a list of words. I remember I was a teacher at that time and I remember I said, "I know that."

You have to remember the times. It was the sixties and we had all this federal money for equipment. Things like a tachistoscope. I used a tachistoscope with kids!

The second thing Ken wrote was that proficient, efficient readers regress to get information and I said, "I knew that, I knew that."

That's the kind of thing that is so good. Ken's research is the kind of research that teachers can understand, because they've lived through listening to kids read real material, and kids trying to tell what they have read.

And what Ken did for us as teachers is give us some insights into why all this is happening. He calls miscue a window on the reading process and that's exactly what I thought when I began to read his work. To this day I teach miscue analysis, and teachers will take that course and they will become researchers, and they gasp sometimes when they get into the miscues and that is what Ken has given us.

Ken's research has made it possible for teachers to be researchers.

Rudine Sims Bishop
Ohio State University

July 6, 1992

I could begin when I met Ken, I was teaching at Morgan State College, it was the time of the NEA grants and someone asked if I would like to go to Texas and I did. And the speakers were Roger Shuy and Ken Goodman, and I had a master's degree and I was looking for a place to do a doctorate. I went to Roger Shuy's presentation and then to Ken's, and Ken put something on the board and asked us about it and then asked how we knew, and I said because Roger Shuy told us yesterday, and Ken laughed, and I liked his sense of humor. I let it be known that I was interested in studying for a doctorate, and I went to Wayne State and studied for a doctorate with Ken.

One of the things that I remember most about Ken is that he ran the place in a fairly democratic way, we would spend mornings or afternoons arguing about miscue and we felt free to argue with him. He wanted the secretaries to call him Ken, and one of the secretaries wouldn't.

I think one of the things that I respected was Ken and Yetta's commitment to real democratic ideals. They sent their kids to public schools. They were committed to the public schools in a place where not everybody was. And I think they were on the forefront of many liberal causes, supporting candidates who they thought would make the right choices. There was a commitment to under-represented kids. Looking at what kids could do rather than a deficit model.

We were invited to their home, and I remember my first Seder. I remember lunches with Ken and Yetta and there was always a group feeling. We had a refrigerator and someone would take responsibility to go and buy salami or whatever and we would make lunch. And we would go to the museum across the street and have lunch. There was a community or family feeling.

As a dissertation advisor Ken was pretty laid back. He was always confident about our abilities. I guess one of the things that I miss of the early days of CELT and when I got out of Wayne were our gatherings when Yetta would play the guitar and Ken and the rest of us would sing. But I feel very much in contact with them, that's one of the special things about Ken and Yetta is that we have kept in touch, I see them at NCTE and IRA.

Yetta was the co-author on my first published article. And it was she who urged us to get involved with NCTE. At their urging they got us to NCTE, and I'm sure it was Yetta who suggested my name for a NCTE committee. And even though the work I am doing now is in children's literature, I was for a long time a Director of a Reading Program at U. Mass., and I introduced a course on psycholinguistics in reading and used miscue analysis as a way of diagnosing children's reading difficulties.

Yetta is always stretching and wondering about new directions. Right now Yetta is always giving me new things to think about.

Ken submitted a program to AERA this year and it was turned down because they said all of the presenters were his students which wasn't true. I think I was the only one who had been one of his students. There is that sense that Ken is a kind of guru and I think that those of us who were his students are a part of that. People see the whole language movement as evangelistic.

I was trying to remember something about his assignments. My memory tells me they were not typical. I know I have a photograph of Ken and me at my graduation with me in my cap and gown. There is one I remember of some of us dressed up for a conference.

Yetta used to talk about her growing up and how her father used to pick up paper and rags, and when she got to be president of NCTE we told her that she was not to tell her paper rags story. When she was president of NCTE she said she was uncomfortable with the suite they gave her at the conference, and she asked how come NCTE was spending money on suites and we told her that the suites were free.

One of my other memories of Yetta is that she could always gather people around her. We would start off going to dinner, there would be four people, me, Dorothy Watson, Dorothy Menosky and Carolyn Burke, and as we moved along Yetta would collect people and by the time we got to dinner there would be ten or twelve people. There are always great conversations when we eat together.

Ira Aaron
University of Georgia

October 21, 1992

I have great respect for Ken but I am not always in agreement with him. He first came to my attention when he was at Wayne State. We met at a conference on psycholinguistics. Then along came the work on miscue.

I know Ken from IRA. Ken was president when I came aboard IRA. I was vice president elect. Jack Cassidy followed Ken and I was after him. It was a time when a number of things occurred. Ralph Staiger was the executive director. He was able to take care of a lot of things that occurred, but just at the time that Ken was president, IRA was beginning to go into the red in their day-to-day operations, mostly because of increased postal rates, and we had to worry about what we did with staff. We had to curtail salary increases for a very good staff.

Ken was very a good president, and when he made his presidential speech I remember there were people sitting in the aisles including some members of his family. It seems to me his grandson may have been down on the floor.

When he presents at IRA his sessions are filled to capacity. I don't ever remember Ken speaking to a small audience.

I had much more contact with Ken than Yetta. I met Yetta later. I remember at one conference Yetta had me look at her number plate of her car, which was MISCUE.

Once we were in Glendale at a conference and Ken had driven a car and was going to return it at the airport, and he couldn't find it and we asked him if he had miscued. Ken has a good sense of humor, a lot of people don't realize that. He is also tolerant. He knows that we don't always agree but it makes no difference.

One little story at the last IRA convention, he was going to discuss whole language and Jeanne Chall was going to discuss phonics. And he said Jeanne was billed as the professor from Harvard and he was billed as the whole language guru.

I think Ken has done a lot of good in bringing these ideas before people. I think he may be more tolerant than some of the people who are his followers. I can't think of anyone who has been more influential in classrooms.

Many teachers need a good bit of structure. I am not one who thinks they have to use a basal reader. I believe children's literature is important, but I believe in more systematic instruction. I think phonics is an important part of learning to read, as is children's literature. Ken would be concerned about the use of basal readers much more than me. Many of the more recent ones you get have very good children's literature.

I've been concerned about Ken's criticism of the excerpting of children's stories in basal readers. I think they have caring editors who sometimes improve on the stories. Sometimes it is good to remove something out of date that may not be appropriate today. Any changes in a basal reader have to be approved by the person who holds the copyright. If Judy Blume is reprinted she has to give her approval.

I can disagree and see the worth, and my disagreements are not that great. The major difference between us is that I would want more structure for teachers, but there is a lot to whole language. Jan Veatch says that whole language is much like the individualized reading that she was advocating in the fifties. Whole language merged language experience with individualized reading.

Ken is diligent and thoughtful and professional. Psycholinguistics, miscue and whole language are all important aspects of his professional life that he is known for not only in US but around the world.

Richard Hodges
University of Chicago

May 18, 1993

My first contact with Ken was in 1967 and he was at Wayne State at that time, and I had come onto the faculty at the University of Chicago. We were both on the program for NCTE and Ken asked if I would like to share a room and so we roomed together. That was the very first time that we met. Ken was getting underway with his work and I had come out of Stanford, and we were the new faces on the block, and people were interested in what we had to say. Dick Venesky was there and Emmett Betts. Emmett contacted the three of us and asked if we would like to come up to his room for cocktails and we got together. We knew what Emmett wanted, which was to pick our brains, and we took a cab to the penthouse at the Hilton, and in an hour Emmett had all the information that he wanted to know.

What ultimately happened was that we all became closer when IRA formed the psycholinguistics committee. Frank Smith was involved and Alan Robinson. This was the first time the reading field had thought about language and we had some good times.

I don't remember the year but the IRA convention was at Atlantic City, and we thought it would be a good idea to have an open committee meeting, and it was put on at six in the evening at the same time as all the publishers parties, and we thought we would have something to eat, and that there would be a few people there, and we went by the room and there were about 1200 people waiting. We decided to have a town meeting and we took questions and answers and it was great.

On the personal side way back then NCTE was held over Thanksgiving, but that meant we were always away from our families and together for Thanksgiving. There must have been at least 16 years when I only had Thanksgiving at home twice. So we got together and Wendy Goodman, Ken and Yetta's daughter, and I have almost the same birthday and so we used to get together and celebrate. They were really marvelous times.

One little thread, I can't tell you the year that this began, it had to be in the early seventies, mainly at IRA and NCTE, as Ken and Yetta began to gather students around them. Ken and Yetta would have hotel room parties and we would sit around and there would be a jug of wine and Yetta would have a guitar. These were before TAWL groups and the same people who were in these early get-togethers were in CELT. They were fun. You could get together and talk. The early days were fun.

I don't have good research for you, but in 1969 the Psycholinguistics Committee sponsored a conference. It may well have been in Chicago. What we did was put together the idea of the importance of language, and the teaching of language, to the importance of reading. The papers out of that conference were so good we decided they were worth publishing, which we did as *Language and Learning to Read: What Teachers Should Know About Language*. I still occasionally get a 50-cent royalty.

But anyway, it was a really important book at the time, because it was one of the first books to bring together theory and practice, and it was one of the forerunners of whole language. There is a section on reading and the researcher-practitioner pair are Ken and Yetta. And what Ken's paper was on was psycholinguistics, and Yetta wrote about miscue analysis. That was a 1970 publication date.

Another thing that relates more closely to Ken, because of the committee, was that we put together a proposal for IRA that we called the travelling road show, that was for researchers and practitioners and we would hold forth on psycholinguistics and reading. Alan Robinson was a member and Dick Venesky. I was there as the language development type, Ken was there as psycholinguistics, Alan Robinson was there as the reading practitioner. IRA sponsored the presentations and that helped people to take it seriously.

We presented in Chicago, LA, New Orleans, and Toronto. The first one was shaky, the second one was better, by the third on we were on a roll, and by the fourth we were jaded.

Another conference at which Ken and I presented was a meeting at the second largest teacher convention in the State of Michigan. It was held in Grand Rapids, and the plan was that there would be four keynoters. Ken was to talk about his work, I was talking, and Roger Shuy was there was to talk about linguistics, and the fourth guy was Ziggy Engelmann, who put together Distar.

Engelmann was a very charismatic guy. He could mesmerize the audience. As you know Distar was completely behavioristic and Ziggy was there to talk about Distar. And they were using it in Detroit, using tokens, and of course doing everything that was antithetical to what Ken believed. Well there were pullout groups and then we all came together, and it is a lesson I will never forget.

We walked in the room that was supposed to hold 250, and

there were 500 people, and they were all Ziggy fans, and whenever we tried to talk there were boos and hisses, and every time Ziggy talked there were cheers, and we were booed out of the auditorium. We were trying to say that what they were getting was surface effects, but they didn't care what it was doing to children, they were concerned with test scores.

It was the first confrontation that I had experienced of a clash of philosophies. Ken is made of sterner stuff than us. We tried to enter the debate but in circumstances like that you don't debate. Engelmann had the upper hand. I remember one of the triggers was that these poor children had no language, and Roger Shuy tried to poke holes in that one. But really we were flabbergasted, because they were saying these children don't know over, and under and up, and down, and that they needed these token programs.

Then when I left Chicago in 1975 and came out to the University of Puget Sound and became Dean, I kept close contact with Ken and Yetta. It is fascinating to watch how Yetta has emerged over time. I have always marveled at her. She has always demonstrated that good people get their work done, and she is not in Ken's shadow. Yetta and I did a thing at the World Congress in Hong Kong. We had some good times together. I think in terms of Ken's presentations, the articulation of his points of view have reached a broader audience because of his relationship with Yetta. I don't think that you can separate the two of them. They are both so sensitive.

Robert Shafer
Arizona State University

June 18, 1992

Let me start with when I first got to know Ken and Yetta, somewhere around 1962 when I left Wayne State to go back to Teachers College. Ken and Yetta arrived in 1962 and I just missed them. But I soon began to hear about Ken's work on psycholinguistics. Ken and I met at IRA in those early days, and then I became aware of Yetta as they developed the reading miscue inventory. The problem with them is that they work so closely together that I don't know which work was Ken's and which was Yetta's.

Now in 1967 I was vice president and program chair of NCTE and I put them on the program, and apparently it was a good opportune time for them to report on the miscue. I think they were on together. I myself became very interested in miscue. Then through Ken and Yetta I became acquainted with Carolyn Burke and Dorothy Watson.

Meanwhile Yetta had got her doctorate, and it was about that time that they moved to Arizona. That was a big move for them.

I was pleased to have them there with that emphasis. I remember that at the U of A you had to have three recommendations for full professor and I was pleased to write for him.

As I said it was hard to know who did what. I remember that they began to make their influence felt very early on, and they weren't affiliated with the Reading Department at the U of A. They also related very quickly to the Arizona social and cultural situation, they began working with Native Americans on reservations.

All this time they were writing and publishing. They began doing international work and became very widely associated with work in reading in the U.K. I had become acquainted with the reading people in the U.K. There is a fearsome woman in the U.K. and she became very upset with the work that Ken and Yetta were doing and publicly attacked them. They had to respond and they responded very well. I remember that this was a big deal in the U.K. It was memorable because the work was just becoming clear in the early seventies.

Ken was given a manuscript to review by someone called Frank Smith and he was amazed by the parallel, and they got together and worked together and although they are temperamentally very different, their work was so closely connected that they worked together for a while. I think a lot of Frank's revisions were influenced by the work of Ken and Yetta. I know Frank would want to make some comments.

Another person whose work was closely related was Jeannette Veatch, she started in the fifties something called Individualized Reading. Individualized Reading was basically the use of trade books and good children's literature. Jeannette Veatch had a really tough time, and Ken and Yetta realized that the work that they were doing supported her position. And Jan saw the implications of Ken and Yetta's work also, and she eventually came to Arizona State and had a lot of communication with Ken and Yetta.

What Ken and Yetta were doing was the first phase of the whole language movement. Carol Edelsky has written that this is a grass roots movement and that's partly true, teachers began to rebel against the skills approach, and they became interested in Ken and Yetta's work.

And then we went through a grass roots time of meeting on Saturdays, designing programs that would integrate reading and writing, but it was only in the early eighties that this began to get into print. Adrian Peetoom worked with Ken on one of the first books, which was called, *What's Whole in Whole Language?*

By this time Ken and Yetta were celebrities.

Meanwhile Yetta published an article on the connection between whole language and progressive education. If you read the Education Act of 1944, the Plowden Report, and the Bullock Report there are really very strong connections. Yetta saw that connection and so we had some talks about that.

I think the thing about both of them is that they have a very broad perspective on curriculum. It comes out in their writing and they continue to be energetically involved in the politics of literacy. Ken and Yetta are both politically active and they don't get upset when people are upset with them.

Two more points, the one thing is that both Ken and Yetta realize that if you have whole language you have to have some way of being accountable, so I think Yetta's work on kid-watching is very significant and their books on whole language assessment are critical.

The other thing is that in the late seventies or eighties, they formed one of the few joint committees between IRA and NCTE, and a lot of interesting things came out of that. There was a publication that came out jointly published by both organizations. It was a three-year committee and we did some fascinating conferences, and out of it came some really significant things. It was either when Yetta was president of NCTE or when Ken was president of IRA.

S. Jay Samuels
University of Minnesota

January 26, 1993

Ken and I were in graduate school together in the 1960's, and we have both won the William S. Gray Award, and he and I are both in the Reading Hall of Fame. So in that sense there is a great deal of overlap in that we have both been recognized by some of the key organizations in reading, and since graduating we have both been in academia.

Ken and I had many opportunities to discuss education.

I think Ken is a really good person, and by that I mean, a good representative of the efforts that were being made to bring psychology out of the era of behaviorism. Remember from 1905 to the 1960's the major paradigm was behaviorism. And one of the things that is important is the paradigm shift that was taking place in the 1950's.

You understand that the goal of behaviorism was such that anything that took place in the head was thought to be unreliable, and therefore psychology only studied observable behaviors.

This had a tremendous impact on education. Nobody studied comprehension except Bartlett, a British psychologist who did interesting work.

So the major research that was going on was on word recognition and not on creativity, thinking, or comprehension. And if you look at psychologists at that time they were looking at word recognition.

Let me see if I can talk about what life was like for Ken Goodman.

My perception is that Ken was on to the psycholinguistic aspects of reading when he was still a graduate student. He had done that study where he gave kids words in isolation and in meaningful contexts and that was his message for many years. There were no political overtones and I have to tell you that Ken was pretty much a lone voice.

Early on I became professionally involved in some of the reading organizations like AERA and Division 15 of the American Psychological Association. And I was asked to put together one and two day workshops for these organizations, and I wanted to put together some meetings with fire and spirit and I would ask Ken and Frank Smith and Joanna Williams. And Ken and Frank presented a very unsettling message to the audience. It was terribly disturbing. The message was that if the child got the meaning it made no difference if the child changed the words.

I remember Joanna getting enraged saying that it makes a difference if the child says, "The man is in jail", if the text says, "The man is in prison", and Ken would say, "No it doesn't".

The audience of psychologists was quiet concerned about transference of text, and knowing how to map was the essence of transfer, and both Frank and Ken were formidable opponents. They both had very well formulated ideas. These were not cranks that were trying to push their ideas down people's throats. They could see the weakness in their opponents' point of view.

You know that Ken recently published something that got me angry. He said that one of the things about his research was that he forced Goff and Samuels to test his ideas. That's not what happened at all. See Ken did not force us to do research. What Ken did was to get us to examine our own positions and our own terminology.

Ken was very clever. He used words like "whole language" and "natural", so you see if you are in a different camp you had to ask, "What camp am I in?" the "half language?" or the "unnatural camp?" On the other hand he also used the term "psycholinguistic approach", that would be a terrible term to use because no one would know what that meant. For a long time Ken did use psycholinguistics and psycholinguists were offended.

Goodman's early years were difficult for him. He probably had more recognition in other countries for example in Australia or New Zealand than the USA. From the period 1965 to the middle 80's his was not a dominant viewpoint, but one that was growing in the USA. Probably by the late 80's it became powerful in the USA.

I'd like to tell a story not about Ken. It's about Frank Smith, but something similar occurred with Ken once. Frank and I were giving a talk at Reed College in Oregon, and I remember presenting an idea at this meeting and Frank saying "Why Jay I really believe that you said something that I agree with." And I said to Frank that our ideas overlapped 90 percent of the time and the same thing happened with Ken.

Again, if you go back to 1965, Ken spans two major psychological periods. Ken comes on the scene during the end period of behaviorism and he comes into the new period of cognitive psychology, when psychologists started studying the comprehension process.

I think if Ken had done his work in the 1920's his work would have been totally ignored, but he comes in at the right time. So Ken comes in at the very moment that the field was ripe. But Ken is not simply telling teachers about how to teach reading, because if you look carefully at Ken's work it is not really very explicit. If you look at Ken's writing it is more of an approach than a specific method. In fact one is hard put to define what whole language is.

Even Ken and Yetta have trouble defining whole language. Harste and Yetta have said if I go into a classroom I can recognize it. Right now I'm doing a study of definitions of whole language and giving the list of definitions to teachers who use other approaches and asking if there is anything unique on the list. For the most part there is not. Except that it is literature based, and I think that there is common agreement that literature based instruction has a lot of good things going for it.

Let me tell you about the future of whole language. I think at the moment whole language is riding a bandwagon of popularity, but whether or not it will remain a dominant force in reading education is whether or not it is an effective way to teach kids to read, and only time will tell. In other words members of state legislators, boards of education, parents and tax payers want to see if they are getting their monies worth. And if they are whole language will be around for a long time and if it turns out it... (Samuels did not finish the sentence.)

It is inconceivable that one method is going to be right for everybody. I wonder about children in lower socioeconomic stations in life. Is it good for children with learning disabilities? And the zeitgeist is such that we are demanding higher levels of literacy. We have literacy inflation going on, so what were considered adequate literate levels a few years ago are no longer high enough.

I would like to know if they have a mission? Was it a clearly articulated mission? When did they get this mission if they had one? How would they evaluate their lives?

I would like to think it is not a shame to dream and not to fulfill all of your dreams. I think life is a failure if you don't have a dream. What was their dream? How do they feel about themselves? They've got to feel pretty good about themselves, and I don't mean because Yetta was president of NCTE and Ken IRA, but the ability to impact the lives of children is a powerful thing.

P. David Pearson
University of California Berkeley

October 5, 1992

Well let's go back to the year 1969 when I was in the last year of graduate school, and I was already aware of Ken in print and his research on the psycholinguistic guessing game. His "Analysis of Oral Reading Miscues: Applied Psycholinguistics," was published in the *Reading Research Quarterly* in the fall of 1969.

He was really a hero for me. There was this researcher who was evoking these views of reading as a language process, which was so refreshing and exciting.

Ken was chair of the psycholinguistics committee for IRA, and I'm a little vague but they had three conferences in a row. The second one was in Kansas City and they were doing a preconvention on psycholinguistics. It was Ken and people like him, and Rudell and Hodges, and I got in to hear these people first hand. It confirmed my convictions that this was the way to go. I talked to Ken about what I was doing in my graduate studies and he was interested and supportive of my work.

So, as is so often the case, conferences give you the opportunity to interact with people whose work is influencing your work. I just felt welcomed into the community. It wasn't just the academic welcome it was the personal welcome.

The next year IRA was at Anaheim and they really went big because many of the same players Ken, Rudell, Hodges and Frank Smith came to that. It was before Frank's book came out and I can remember what a wonderful complement Frank's work was to Ken's. By that time I had finished my degree and Ken saw to it that I got on that committee that next year. I cannot tell you what a difference that meant to my career that Ken got me onto the committee.

I still don't think I met Yetta then. I have a vivid recollection of Yetta coming to a meeting at IRA, and I remember her coming up to me after my talk saying that this is an important message and you need to get it published, and I still hadn't published my dissertation and they kept encouraging me. Making sure I submitted it.

Let me back up and talk about the importance of Ken's ideas. To me in 1968-69 what I found so powerful in his message, from a humanistic perspective, was giving kids credit for what they do. He was trying to understand what they took away from the printed page in terms of what they took to it. To me that would be a germ of an idea that would grow into a model of comprehension. Sounds transparent now, but back then it was not so obvious.

So Ken helped us from a humanistic perspective as well as a cognitive perspective. There is an incredible intellectual depth to the writing that Ken was doing. Like the psycholinguistic guessing game.

It must have been in the early 1970' when I got introduced to the CELT network. I'm talking about people like Ken and Yetta, and also Rudine Sims, Bill Page and Jerry Harste, and even though

I wasn't a part of it, they always made me feel welcome. And the CELT network was really important to me, for even though I wasn't a part of it, it was with that group that I debated intellectual issues. I can't begin to tell you the number of hours that people like Ken and Jerry and I spent arguing with one another.

It was CELT that, even though I wasn't a part of it, that helped me define who I was. We always have to define what we know in relation to other things. And through all the years, I think I have continued to sort of define myself in relationship to the Goodmans' agenda, and in the last decade that has come to mean not only Ken, but Yetta's perspective also. I think particularly her work on print awareness. What I have always respected in them, even though we don't see eye to eye on issues, is that they would always listen to what I have to say.

Let's take an obvious issue like phonics. I think we would agree that kids need to learn the grapho-phonemic system and it becomes an important resource that they have in their tool kit. I think that they would question whether or not it should be taught. They would say it needs to be learned but not taught, and I would say I am more sanguine about teaching.

I think one of the crimes is that once we started testing it – all the silly tests made us teach phonics more directly.

Another difference between us is that I am a little more sanguine about approaching parts of the instructional process directly. I am less worried about explicit instruction. I advocate modeling and demonstration, but I think I am in a very different place than I was 5 or 6 years ago. I think back then I would have said you can decontextualize, now I'm more suspicious.

If you try to teach for the general case you just get a bunch of garbage.

It is much more important to support what children are doing at hand, and in the process help them realize the generalizability. I find myself changing a lot. I think on the issue of explicit teaching we do differ.

There is another kind of respect for Ken and Yetta. I've tried to be a real student of the whole language movement. I think the difference is a political difference, I am much more interested in consensus. I am a member of the radical middle.

I really am concerned that the field reaches for consensus on what we do agree on. And I think I would be more willing to compromise a principle along the way and I don't think that is an indictment of them or me.

The other thing you have to know is that I feel close to them personally. Whenever I see Yetta we are all hugs. Whatever the differences, we have incredible respect for one another. Ken too. I don't want to miss that, beyond my respect for their work, I have this incredible respect for what they do for children and teachers, and for the passion with which they approach that task. And even though I would not do things the way they do, I have incredible respect for them for that.

The personal support has been overwhelming for me over the years, and they have provided that kind of intellectual support. If I talk with Yetta about an issue she always has seven people that I should talk to. There is a wonderful balance between their personal and professional contributions to the field.

Roger Shuy
Georgetown University

October 13, 1992

I am trying to think of the beginning point, about 1965, I might be off a year, when Ken gave a paper at a conference in Boston, I believe it was IRA, but it could have been NCTE, and I gave a paper. I had read his article on the psycholinguistic guessing game. As it turned out he gave his paper about an hour before I gave mine. I sat in the audience and my heart sank, because he said exactly what I was going to say. I went up afterwards and met him and I told him I was embarrassed, because I going to give a paper that was basically the same, and he said it didn't make any difference as the audience needed to hear it over and over again. And I felt very close to him, because I was coming towards reading and he was coming towards linguistics, and we were treading in each other's territories.

But it didn't make any difference and we tried to help each other. I had got involved in reading about the time my oldest son was in elementary school and having difficulty reading, and I went into his elementary school and his teacher said he couldn't identify syllables. His teacher was calling any sound with a vowel in it a syllable, and I asked her about "lemon", and she said that my son had only identified one syllable. I explained that was probably because he only heard one vowel sound "lemn".

I began to look at reading and the ways in which it was being taught didn't make sense. The importance given to syllabification was fairly silly. And that's how I got involved in writing about reading, and I found myself being hired by Ginn trying to make sense out of their work, and all the time I was discussing this with Ken and Yetta, and I think we had a fairly common beginning point, which was that kids were a whole lot smarter than we give them credit for.

Over the years we have had some arguments, especially over decoding, but we had 99 percent agreement. I think Ginn and all publishers had way over done it with phonics and decoding. And it occurred to me that linguistics had a whole lot more to say about reading than about decoding.

The next memory has to do with their project on miscue, when they had the first grant and I consulted with them. I remember having long discussions with them about error, and I think I might have been responsible for their problem with the word error. And I really liked the way they were going at that time.

For the first time teachers were able to find out some things about reading that were more than "you are doing this wrong." The big contribution was to distinguish the difference between reading errors and the normal production of language.

Ken and I did a number of conferences at the same time, and on one occasion we plotted ahead of time that I would take the educator's position and he would take the linguist's position. It was a test of each other's ability. I am a linguist by training, but I'm a different kind of linguist in that I think the higher calling is that we need to be able to apply linguistics to understand the real world. Which explains why I have been involved with linguistics and the law.

I got pretty disenchanted with the reading field and I really admire Ken and Yetta for sticking to it. The field has so many long-held beliefs about reading. Phonics is pretty goofy. I don't think I had the clout being an outsider and I don't have the patience that they have. I mentioned that I was at Ginn and it got so bad in the last few years that all they would listen to was the market place, and I began to feel like a fifth wheel. Ginn was bought by Xerox. I'm not sure what happened after that.

When Ken and Yetta moved to Arizona I lost contact. I don't belong to IRA anymore. Ken and Yetta ask me to visit. I remember I once did a book on linguistics and reading that was the result of a conference that I held at the Linguistics Society of America, because I thought linguists should know more about reading. We did a session which was then repeated at IRA.

The IRA program had a linguist and then an educator and then actual classroom teachers. The linguist would present a linguist concept, the educator would take it and talk its function in reading education, and then the teacher would talk about use in the classroom. The problem was that I couldn't get the teachers to write anything.

The paradox is that a good idea has to have a name and an identity, but then once that happens, the name and identity become close to theology in the eyes of some.

I was really happy when Ken and Yetta went to Arizona and I remember talking to them about our personal contributions. We said that if we looked back at some time in our lives we hoped there would be fifty or a hundred graduate students who took what we did and took it further and I think that is one of the great contributions of their lives.

Some people are Yetta supporters and some are Ken supporters, but I don't know how you separate them. One of my great regrets is that we never worked together on any projects. I read their proposals. But we never co-authored anything.

I guess I would like to know more about them. Read an unravelling from whatever state of innocence they began. I'd like to hear about the things that got in the way. I would like to see the struggle against the opposition. How they have dealt with the old guard's inability to change. In education there is a lot of talk about change and then it's gone. I wonder how they have managed in light of an absolutely entrenched field. Education is built on an agricultural model and has been used to warehouse kids.

Jerome Harste
Indiana University

September 17, 1992

The one thing I do want to say is that I am not a student of Ken's in a formal sense, but I am in an academic sense. I would like to know Ken's thinking more, but you only get that from day to day conversations.

All my stories involve relationships with other people.

One of my favorite stories is when they were at Wayne State doing miscue and trying to develop taxonomies. They were developing categories and then deciding whether they were contributing to the theory. Ken walked in one day and decided he was going to drop intransitive verbs and Dorothy Menosky said but you can't drop them, I have gone and coded all these intransitive verbs.

A moderately humorous point is that I got introduced to Ken through David Pearson. David and I were graduate students together. We used to get together. David said. "Harste you've just got to read this article, 'Reading, a Psycholinguistic Guessing Game.'" That was when I was finishing my master's degree.

I have been interested in psycholinguistics ever since. It was ten years before I understood it, and that was thanks to Carolyn Burke. Working with Carolyn was like getting a second doctorate.

Another story I guess I could tell is the story of Ken learning my name. I had been introduced to Ken several different times and he never remembered my name. We saw him at IRA and Carolyn said, "Let me introduce you," and I said, "You have introduced me seven times and he never remembers my name, I'll just use his work," and I think Carolyn took him aside.

Ken has made some statements that have held up for a very long time, that have had tenure longer than most ideas. I think it is his insight into language and the reading process that have stood up over time. I don't know any principles of learning that have held up as well.

In Chicago he was masterful at taking on mastery learning. He pulled out workbook pages and on one page were two left feet, and Ken said it was a program of two left feet.

Ken said, "How come that there are no good examples of mastery learning?"

He really showed that mastery learning does not translate into practice. That was one of the most powerful learning experiences of my own. I ask Ken why he was so feisty. He said, "I refuse to leave misinformation on the floor."

That caused a good deal of reflection on my part. I don't think we should respond to everything, but we do have a responsibility to respond to misinformation.

I like the principle.

I think it is his ability to take an individual instance to a broader frame that has always impressed me.

The other thing that I have always liked about Ken is the way he responds to questions. In many ways Ken is not like one of these people. He is not a jackrabbit. He really takes the time to build background information. I think what makes him a marvelous teacher, you accidently learn a lot about language from just being in his presence. You just pick it up. I think by answering questions in a complete fashion, you get a whole different understanding of an issue.

His policy is one of extended elaboration.

I heard Ken speak at the Whole Language Umbrella, and he had been working on an update of his new model and I think it is interesting to see what he is willing to incorporate in his model.

His early models were pretty psycholinguistic. He didn't take into account context. It was language and thought, not really sociolinguistic. In some ways I was disappointed because he seemed to be rejecting a sociolinguistic model, but now he has incorporated the view.

I haven't been so successful with semiotics. You always got a sense that he knew what it is that he needed still to work on. You get a strong theoretical sense, and in many ways what he included has contributed to the theoretical argument, so you always know what work you have to do.

When I look at what his contributions are, I think my own feeling is that he has given us a new research methodology. I'm not sure that his psycholinguistic theory is his real contribution. Ken asks, "Well what's there, that's where we have to start," and that's where Yetta, Dorothy, and Carolyn come in.

His real contribution is he anchored himself in building

grounded theory, working with what is there. Watching real language in use. Graves did it in writing and Halliday in oral language.

Ken really started a revolution. What is the kid trying to do? If we really understood that and then ask, "How can we support the kid?" I think Ken had his finger on it. We ought to be working for the improvement of curricula experiences. How can I set up environments that support what kids are trying to do?

Ken is a carefully principled person. I think the essence of his work is the ethical and the moral dimensions that we haven't explored. I'm defining moral as the kinds of values that bind relationships between teachers and children. His new perspective is really a shift that has moral implications that are fundamental to the way in which we view foundations of education.

The fundamental shift that Ken has brought about is that things that aren't data are data. It comes back to the story of mastery learning with their test-retest. It's no good to explain 100 kids research, when we can't explain one. If cases aren't data then there is no data. What they call "data" is numbers, not data.

It is failing to understand the basic relationship between teachers and kids that anyone who doesn't want to look at "cases" doesn't understand. I think it is this realization that helps us get to what is really basic is what Ken is really good at.

I haven't said much about Yetta, but Yetta has contributed the practical. It doesn't mean I don't think that Yetta is not theoretical. That's the wedding, the bringing of the theory and practical together. Yetta, Rudine Sims, Dorothy Watson, and Dorothy Menosky are living proof of why we need collaborators.

If the theory doesn't do anything then it isn't much of a theory. To understand Ken is to understand the relationships between theory and practice, which he and Yetta have done through the whole language movement.

Angela Jaggar
New York University

November 12, 1992

It is an interesting thing, I feel like I've always known them. I guess it was back in the 1970's I really got to know Yetta through the Impact Conferences. Yetta was energetic, dynamic, and supportive, all at the same time. She was wonderful at getting people to do things.

Each of the four Impact Conferences had a slightly different focus. And a lot of people began to realize that the findings of the research that the presenters were talking about could be used in their classrooms. At about the end of the second conference we had gotten a lot of responses about kid-watching, and I said we ought to have some kid-watching workshops, and Yetta said, "Why don't you do it?"

And we went on to incorporate kid-watching workshops in the Impact Conferences. It actually became the Impact Conferences in 1979, which was the UN Year of the Child, and was the introduction of many researchers and teachers to the research of Michael Halliday, also to Marie Clay's work, and to the work of Moira McKenzie.

We also started looking for teachers who were doing these kinds of things. We wanted them to be speakers, and for the third and fourth Impact Conference we set it up that way.

There are a few other exciting things that came out of the Impact Conferences. We began networking. It was an effort, as I saw it, to high-light and learn more about the exciting work that was being done all over the world in studying language from different perspectives.

There was so much that came out of the Impact Conferences. It was very exhilarating. There was a core group of people and then others. IRA was much more amenable because of their structure than NCTE. We had trouble with NCTE, with the Executive Committee. They would always meet when programs were taking place.

At the second Impact Conference, Yetta came up to me and said, "Well Angela, I can't get out of the executive meeting, will you chair the conference?"

If I had to pick one person who everybody related to through those conferences it would be Yetta. They were challenging times. There was always time for dialogue. Exciting ideas about child development were coming out and we needed to talk.

Papers from the Impact Conferences were compiled by Yetta, Myna Haussler, and Dorothy Strickland. *Oral and Written Language Development Research Impact on Schools* is available through ERIC. It does include Michael Halliday's paper "Three Aspects of Children's Language Development" that has been widely circulated.

Then there was the book *Observing the Language Learner*, which was the one that Trika Smith-Burke and I put together. It is the only book co-published by IRA and NCTE and that was Yetta's idea again. I don't think that people realize the connections between the two organizations Yetta made.

At the end of the four Impact Conferences we did some small conferences. At that time IRA's grants for small conferences were available, and Dorothy Watson organized a conference in Missouri, Dorothy Strickland and I organized one in New York, and there was one on the West Coast.

Then the Impact Conference Committee turned into the Strategies Committee. The idea was to have collaboration. The Strategies Conferences looked at implementation and making change. They were the extension of taking this work and looking at the implications for practice.

I'm not sure if it was part of the Strategy Conferences, but we put together a pre-convention at IRA, and we had Vera John-Steiner, Vito Perrone and Emelia Ferreiro together – that was Yetta.

One of the challenges was to give teachers voice. We were trying to change the ways in which we worked and talked. More and more committees were interested in interacting. In the midst of all this whole language burst on the scene and my perspective is that the whole language movement came out these meetings.

The TAWL Groups were started.

The exciting thing is that people became familiar with whole language from different disciplines. We were very anxious to get more of a social perspective.

We also learned at that time how hard it was to get administrators to come to conferences like this. But in many respects it was very exciting because we did get many people. For me it was like a world opening up. It was 1977 or 1978 and it was so exciting because there was so much going on with oral language.

Yetta and I have talked about broader issuers of curriculum, and it was very exciting to hear Martha King. Every time she spoke everyone listened. The wonderful thing was that her perspective was broader because she had been an administrator.

Ken and Yetta are always networking. They are not off in the ivory tower. They are not people who are just behind pages.

Barbara Flores
California State University

August 25 and September 13, 1992

I'll start with stories of different things that I know. I was getting my masters at Sacramento and I ran across Ken's writing and I saw passion and compassion in Ken's writing for kids. I had a professor who said I should go on and get my doctorate and it was a real dilemma. And my kids asked me if I was going to teach teachers the way that you teach us and I said, "Yes", and they said I should go.

I was recruited by Harvard and Stanford and I went and talked to a professor at Berkeley, and he said we used to be the best, but the best is where the Goodmans are at the University of Arizona, and so I took a trip, and I applied, and was accepted.

And I remember showing up at Ken's doctoral seminar and Ken asked everyone why they were there. And he asked me and I said, "I came to study with you," and he said, "You what? Why didn't you write?" and I said, "I didn't write because I don't know you", and I said, "If after a year you don't think I'm worthy you can tell me," and Ken laughed, and then a year later they kicked Ken and

Yetta out of the Reading Department, and I was Ken's student so that was a tight rope to walk.

But they were the ones, Ken and Yetta, they got us involved in conferences, they brought in Michael Halliday and Don Graves, and they got us involved. In elementary the students who studied with them shared and collaborated with them. I said, "These are real genuine people." My father said, "You watch what people do, not what they say", and Ken and Yetta are very consistent. They do what they say. We were starving graduate students and they had us over two or three times a week. Besides the work we were doing in class we would read and talk about what we were reading, thinking about logical consequences. They spent a lot of time mentoring us. They just devoted a lot of time -- it was just incredible the amount of time with us.

Ken has a more Socratic approach to teaching. Yetta has a different style she would take opposite positions. I had always wondered why phonics is such an issue, and Ken told me "You're going to figure that out". And I went and read all that I could about the history of phonics, and I guess what I learned was how to argue and think about the epistemology, and when I had doubts about myself they would be there. And talk about the pot calling the kettle black, Yetta would say, "You need to learn not to be so aggressive", and I would say, "Look at yourself", and she'd say not to be so caustic, and then she would say to a student "That's not the way to do it!" and then she would add "That's not the way to do it! I lost control."

Ken expected you to do a lot of reading. I was the first Latina, first Mexican American, to study with them, and I remember Yetta saying, "You are going to be a leader. You have a lot of responsibility for your people's history."

And I remember I went to my first Seder, and I started to cry and I said I can't believe that your religion is based on fairness. I remember crying. I remember I guess just the genuine humanity and drive that they have. It's unending. I remember just getting exhausted. The energy is just amazing to me, and this is all over the world and I was amazed by that. And both of them have such vision they challenged their students, and it's in terms of what they see, and they see potential in all the students.

And in terms of just politics and I guess preparing us. I should speak for myself they prepared me as far as scholarship. The one thing I didn't expect, I thought, "Now I have my doctorate", but I wasn't prepared for what I met, which was a lot of antagonism. I remember calling them up and saying, "I don't know if it's because I am Hispanic or a woman or one of your students", and Ken said, "Try all three Barbara."

The network through CELT has been very important. You know what is very interesting is that Yetta will bring people into her house, and I would say, "Yetta why do you bring them into the house when you know they will stab you in the back?" And Yetta would say, "But I will not be like them." They have dedicated much of their lives to teachers and they are unrelenting in their advocacy, and I guess I was attracted to them because I thought there was hope being a Latino for them to debunk the status quo which was very important.

Let's see, I said that they do this with all the graduate students. They see strengths and push us and take us with them in any context that they are in. And I remember Ken saying when he was going to be president of IRA that we have to bring in Latin America and other countries. And he was invited to go to Argentina, Uruguay, and Chile, and he said we need a translator. They paid for my lodging and I paid for my flight. We met different groups in Uruguay and Argentina.

In Argentina it was just after the revolution and professors had to have three jobs to pay basic bills. They asked us not to ask them about the political situation. They asked us not to ask them. Right from the first they asked us not to ask any questions. We met with professors and they had read things and they wanted Ken and Yetta to clarify, and Karen (their daughter) and I were translating all day long.

When Ken gave speeches the translators would change every fifteen minutes. Isn't that amazing? And Ken would give us long sections of his talks, and we would have to say we need smaller chunks, and we had to find a rhythm and a cadence.

Uruguay was more impressive. Ken gave a talk in an auditorium and you couldn't see the people, and Ken kept talking, and I was trying to keep up, and we asked if there was someone who could take over, and a woman in the audience took over. What was interesting was that the people that had invited Ken to come were from the upper class, and when they found out my background they stopped talking to me. They had assumed that I was upper class, because I was working on my doctorate.

Then we went back to Buenos Aires and on to Bahia Blanca and I was very comfortable. Those people were very kind and very grateful that Ken had gone there and it didn't matter what class you came from. They were thirsty for knowledge and they had read Ken's work.

In Uruguay people were very deficit driven and Ken kept raising issues. By contrast in Bahia Blanca they wanted to move out of that model. They were interested in the way in which miscues show strengths as well as weaknesses. There was an incident going back to Buenos Aires. I was sitting with Ken and Karen, and the military on the plane made me go and sit at the back of the plane with the military. Ken said, "She is with us", and they said, "No she has to sit with us", and I played dumb, and these men were pilots and they were talking about all their missions.

Then we went to Chile and getting off the plane was scary. We had soldiers pointing machine guns at us and we were backed up against this wall. Then some officials arrived and we didn't even have to go through customs. We were so frightened.

In Chile Ken gave talks and they had hired translators, and by then Ken was a lot better. He had found his cadence and he gave smaller chunks and it went very well. And we talked to professors and Karen and I spent a lot of time negotiating meaning in small groups as professors asked them questions about their work.

Their work has had impact in these countries. Ken said, "I imagined it could happen, but I didn't expect it to happen so soon." He said he was glad that he had gone to Latin America even though it was a risky trip.

Oh I didn't tell you this, when we first got off the plane in Buenos Aires, we were mobbed and people were trying to take our suitcases. And I said, "We don't know who all these people are," and Ken said, "We are going to have to use our intuition", and finally we picked someone. And you know he is Jewish and there was a lot of anti-Semitism.

I also remember that he brought in Emilia Ferreiro. Do you know how significant it is to bring in women of color who are pioneers? Ken and Yetta did that. I think their work has really been revolutionary throughout the world.

I know that their students have gone on to be leaders and pioneers in the field. We gave a talk last year and Yetta came up in tears and hugged us, and she said, "I know the future is safe with you".

Wherever we go we build support with students and teachers. We build community. We value the social lives of people. I think though what has shocked people is that whole language is a political movement.

One of my students I had two years ago was from Argentina, and she said to me, "Barbara, do you realize what whole language is?" and I said, "Yes, it is very political," and she said, "Yes. And that is why we had a revolution in Argentina, because we had become too critical."

Ken and Yetta have always been there when I needed them, but I wasn't prepared for the racism and prejudice at that level. Getting a doctorate and doing research means breaking into a system that has never accepted Latina women. Before I used to get depressed, now I step out of it and think what to do.

I guess that is part of being a leader. I know that Ken and Yetta have suffered a lot in the academy, both because of their positions, and because they are Jewish. And yet Yetta will embrace her enemies. She used to tell me, "I will not be like them".

Bess Altwerger
Towson University

September 15, 1992

Where do I start? I went to hear Ken and Yetta and Dorothy at a conference, and I asked Ken who I should study with for a master's degree, and he said, Dorothy Menosky, and that is what I did.

I really had no intentions of getting a doctorate, but Dorothy thought I should do that, and she phoned Ken and before I knew it I was on a plane to Arizona. I was very nervous. I had great doubts that I would make it as a graduate student, but there were many things about Ken and Yetta that gave me the courage and the confidence in myself.

Yetta and Ken were important to me on many levels. When I went out there it was very comforting to me that these people came from a working back background as I did, and they had a similar cultural background as myself. And Yetta was particularly significant and I immediately related to her. I sensed that our upbringings were very similar, and I felt if Yetta could succeed then somehow I could, and I watched her in terms of how she bridged the gap between her culture and the academic culture. I really truly don't know if I would have been able to succeed in academia if it wasn't for the confidence I gained from working with Yetta.

So I went out to Arizona and they welcomed me into their family. At that time their girls had left for college, and it was the first time I had been away from my family, I know they had a parental role towards me, and there was a feeling of security that I gained from knowing that they were there.

It took me a while to talk to them, to call Ken, Ken and not Dr. Goodman. We really filled a lot of roles. It was a very complex relationship. At times it was difficult when you wanted one role to take over, it was difficult to get rid of the other roles. There were times when I wanted to get rid of the child-adult relationship and become colleagues, and there was a struggle around that. There was a collegial student relationship and parental relationship, and it was difficult to keep all of this going.

Yetta and Ken worked together and it was amazing watching them. They had offices next to each other and then they went home together. And I saw Yetta change. At the beginning Yetta was the practitioner and Ken the theorist, but she changed over the years. I have never known a couple like the Goodmans or a family. They were working class in their roots, but they were also intensely intellectual. I have never seen a couple who worked together like this that argued theory and politics. I guess I learned as much from them as people, as I learned of them as academics.

I was always impressed by their sense of political awareness. They were intensely anti-racist. I had been around political awareness, but Ken and Yetta had a real solid understanding of who they were. I would spend hours just debating politics with them. We would argue about linguistics, Chomsky versus Halliday.

One thing that I think was really important was the sense of community that they developed in their graduate students. You didn't have a sense of competition. I always felt lucky to be a part of that. There were students from Australia and Canada. Ken and Yetta ushered us in, and in some programs I don't think that would have happened. They never fostered competition between us.

Another thing Ken and Yetta would invite people from all over the country and their graduate students. We did have a chance to meet all these people.

Ken and Yetta were wonderful from the very beginning at getting us involved in conferences, and they introduced us to the academic world. They let us camp out in their hotel rooms. When they got these suites we would move in with them and camp out on the floor. They would help us with the proposals and they would critique us.

They got us involved in CELT and through conferences and CELT we almost instantly became a part of the extended family with Dorothy Watson, Rudine Sims, and Jerry Harste. It was an incredible way to enter the academic world.

I remember going to Indiana and Ken presented his newest version of the model, and I remember having a debate with Ken and Carolyn Burke. She didn't treat me as a graduate student. They never talked down to you. They always talked to you on the same level.

I've met many many people, who have had a feeling of isolation in the academic world, in programs where their mentors did not mentor them. What was really neat was that we met the Indiana students who worked with Jerry and Carolyn Burke, and I have long-lasting friendships with students from Indiana. What we saw was the way in which they would argue amongst themselves, and we learned you can have a lively debate in which there is room for dialogue and disagreement.

I think that is the reason that the research continues to grow. To this day Ken and Yetta are non-stop learners. Learning is an exciting adventure. It always amazes me that after all these years they are still pursuing interesting intellectual ideas. I think that is true of their whole intellectual community.

I cannot imagine Ken and Yetta retiring from their intellectual life. I can imagine them giving up their jobs, but not intellectual life.

One thing you learn when you work with Ken and Yetta is that they are tireless. They are very demanding of themselves, and they set very high expectations for themselves. When you are mentored by people like that, the expectations that they set for you are incredibly high. It has taken me years to allow myself not to work all the time. When you are around a Yetta Goodman who never stops, I always feel I should be doing research, and that has been a struggle for me, setting my expectations too high, and balancing my life, and not feeling I have to live up to their expectations for themselves.

Ken and Yetta had very high expectations for their graduate students. Coming out of the university as Goodman students you felt you had to put out spectacular dissertations. Both Barbara Flores and I really struggled. Neither of us knew how to write. I wrote a chapter of my dissertation that I thought was wonderful, and I expected them to think it was wonderful, and they thought it was awful, and they helped me and it was a very difficult process.

The minute I arrived in Arizona they got me involved in two research projects. I collected data for the print awareness studies. The proposal and funding had already been approved, but Yetta had me right in there working on it and she had me presenting on the print awareness study almost as soon as I arrived. I was amazed that people were interested in finding out what I knew, and that was because they knew that Ken and Yetta really involved their students.

The other study was a dialect study with Ken, and I was involved in writing up some of the data, and I developed some computer programs for running the data through. I really learned how to do research. They always made sure that they had positions for their students and they supported us financially. I certainly couldn't have afforded to get a doctorate.

Oh I have lots of stories about consulting. Barbara and I had to drive for nine hours to get to the Navajo Reservation. For fifty dollars a day we'd stay for three or four days. We would stay at the one motel with no phone, to work with the students. Ken and Yetta came with us a few times, and I watched them very carefully and then they sent us out on our own.

You know Ken was also pretty tough. He was always amazed at how provincial I am. Well Ken and Yetta knew I was this New York City kid who had hardly ever been out of NYC. Once Barbara and I were on our way to the Navajo Reservation, and it was snowing and we stopped at Flagstaff, and in the morning there was a lot of snow, and we phoned Ken and told him we were not going on, and I know he was not pleased, because if you make a commitment you keep it.

I often think about where they fit in historically. Why Ken and Yetta were able to develop the theories as they did, and how their theories on reading will impact the future for teachers and kids.

Other Books By Ken Goodman

Forthcoming Garn Press Books by Ken Goodman

The Smart One: A Grandfather's Tale. (2015)

Other Books by Ken Goodman

Whose Knowledge Counts in National Literacy Policies?: Why Expertise Matters (edited book, with Robert Calfee and Yetta Goodman). (2013)

Reading in Asian Languages: Making Sense of Written Texts in Chinese, Japanese, and Korean (edited book, with Shaomei Wang, Meiko Iventosch, and Yetta Goodman). (2012)

Scientific Realism in Studies of Reading (edited book with Alan Flurkey and Eric Paulson). (2007).

The Truth About DIBELS: What It Is - What It Does. (2006)

Saving Our Schools: The Case for Public Education, Saying No To "No Child Left Behind" (edited book, with Yetta Goodman, Patrick Shannon, and Roger Rapoport). (2004)

On the Revolution of Reading: The Selected Writings of Kenneth S. Goodman (edited book of by Alan Flurkey and Jingguo Xu of selected Goodman articles). (2003)

In Defense of Good Teaching (edited book). (1998)

On Reading. (1996)

Studies In Miscue Analysis: An Annotated Bibliography (edited book). (1996)

Basal Readers, A Second Look (with Patrick Shannon). (1994)

Phonics Phacts. (1994)

The Game Of Chess. (1992)

Organizing for Whole Language (with Yetta Goodman and Wendy Hood). (1991)

The Whole Language Catalog (with Lois Bird and Yetta Goodman). (1991)

The Whole Language Catalog: Supplement on Authentic Assessment (with Lois Bird and Yetta Goodman). (1992)

The Whole Language Catalog: Forms for Authentic Assessment (with Lois Bird and Yetta Goodman). (1993)

The Whole Language Evaluation Book (with Yetta Goodman and Wendy Hood). (1988)

Language and Thinking in School: A Whole-Language Curriculum (with E. Brooks Smith, Robert Meredith and Yetta M. Goodman). (1986)

What's Whole in Whole Language. (1986)

> French edition (1986); Spanish edition (1989); Japanese edition (1990); Portuguese edition (1997); Chinese edition (1998); 20th Anniversary edition (2005)

Report Card on Basal Readers (with Patrick Shannon, Yvonne Freeman and Sharon Murphy). (1988)

Language and Literacy: The Selected Writings of Kenneth S. Goodman. (Edited and Introduced by Frederick V. Gollasch). (1982)

Linguistics, psycholinguistics, and the teaching of reading: An annotated bibliography. (1980)

Reading In The Bilingual Classroom: Literacy And Biliteracy. (1979)

Miscue Analysis: Applications to Reading Instruction. (1973)

The Psycholinguistic Nature Of The Reading Process with A New Foreword (edited book). (1973)

www.ingramcontent.com/pod-product-compliance
Lightning Source LLC
Chambersburg PA
CBHW051536020426
42333CB00016B/1948